THE TWELVE DOORWAYS
TO HEALING

America's beloved spiritual healer, Ruth Carter Stapleton, shares with you the twelve most important stepping stones to health—

love ★ faith ★ surrender ★ forgiveness
confession ★ self-acceptance ★ release
purpose ★ serving ★ listening ★ adversity
authentic self-identity

Now, you can learn how to master these twelve lessons so that you, too, can live a life of peace, happiness and Christian love.

Bantam Books by Ruth Carter Stapleton

THE EXPERIENCE OF INNER HEALING
THE GIFT OF INNER HEALING

THE EXPERIENCE OF INNER HEALING

Ruth Carter Stapleton

*This low-priced Bantam Book
has been completely reset in a type face
designed for easy reading, and was printed
from new plates. It contains the complete
text of the original hard-cover edition.*
NOT ONE WORD HAS BEEN OMITTED.

THE EXPERIENCE OF INNER HEALING

*A Bantam Book / published by arrangement with
Word, Inc.*

PRINTING HISTORY

*Word Books edition published June 1977
2nd printing .... November 1977
Bantam edition / January 1979*

Cover photograph by Larry B. Stevenson

ISBN 0-553-12047-6

This book may not be reproduced in whole or in part, by mimeograph or any other means, without permission. For information address: Word, Inc., 4800 West Waco Drive, Waco, Texas 76703

Published simultaneously in the United States and Canada

Bantam Books are published by Bantam Books, Inc. Its trademark, consisting of the words "Bantam Books" and the portrayal of a bantam, is Registered in U.S. Patent and Trademark Office and in other countries. Marca Registrada. Bantam Books, Inc., 666 Fifth Avenue, New York, New York 10019.

PRINTED IN THE UNITED STATES OF AMERICA

Contents

Foreword

Many sincere and intelligent Christians mistrust psychology. They have "abided in Jesus Christ" enough to know that he is the Source of their life. When secular psychology claims that there is no need for "the spiritual," that emotional integrity is everything, that emotional integration is man's goal, they rebel; they know that such claims are lopsided, ignorant and false. Many of these deeply committed people have written off psychology as irreverent and irrelevant.

On the other hand, growing numbers of sincere seekers have found emotional healing through the discipline of psychology. These people have also learned that Jesus Christ can enter their lives and instill a sense of peace, love and power they have never known before which is obviously not a product of psychological therapy.

What has emerged in the last decade is a recognition that both of these positions have great truth. A further revolutionary discovery spotlights Jesus' teaching that nothing is secular, that every day, every person, every principle rooted in truth and life is sacred, therefore spiritual. Dedicated Christians have "discovered" the corollary truth that even psychology is filled with insights and concepts that are spiritual—though they are found in a "secular" context. The ministry of inner healing attempts to bring authentic principles of psychology under the guidance and inspiration of the Holy Spirit. When this happens, people are healed, new ministers of inner healing are raised up, and the entire redemptive movement increases in quantum measure.

This statement does not imply that God has no use for ministers who ignore psychology, or psychologists who ignore the spiritual nature of their work. Rather, it is to say that the majority of people need greater wholeness than they have experienced under one leadership or the other, and that each discipline needs the insights of the other. To be led through secular psychological disciplines by the Holy Spirit is to be led into the experience of emotional healing. And this means that one is reconstructed by the Holy Spirit of God.

Introduction

Inner healing is a process of emotional reconstruction experienced under the guidance of the Holy Spirit. It is not an attempt to supplant psychiatry or to ignore the wisdom found in secular psychology. Historically the church has recognized Jesus Christ as the great physician; his message and Spirit have inspired the development of medical and psychiatric science as well as the spiritual exercise of praying for miraculous physical healing. Inner healing of emotional trauma is the logical, natural extension of this same inspiration.

In the first public message of his ministry, Jesus said that he not only came to heal the physically ill, but "those who are downtrodden, bruised, crushed and broken down by calamity."[1] Clearly this is his public pronouncement of God's commission to him: his task is that of inner healing which alone can release the heart from the emotional shadows and the trauma that keep the "crushed and broken" bound to their past calamities.

We live in the "future shock" world of rapid change. The discoveries being made in the physical world from atom bombs to DNA molecules are revolutionizing our lives and thinking. Even more significant discoveries in the emotional and spiritual world have begun to emerge. Not the least of these is inner healing. But the discipline of inner healing suffers the same fate as valid new insights in many fields, which appear at first exposure to be impractical novelties. Scriptural references, however, strongly infer that inner healing was a part of God's redemptive intention during the apostolic age. While "inner healers" may not have used some of our modern psychological terminology, it is probable that our terminology is what makes old methods and insights appear to be new. And this new language may, in turn, make methods suspect. But an intimate association with the process of inner healing for even a short time will prove to all but the prejudiced that inner healing is a process which deserves our acceptance and warrants its expanded use.

The sick heart is described by Jesus as the source of every human defiling wickedness.[2] The converse implication is that the healed heart is the cornucopia of every human blessing. This is why no discovery in the laboratory, no innovation in the political arena, not even a new proclamation from the church sanctuary is as important as healing the heart through successfully dealing with the person's past.

Faith-imagination, the primary tool of this discipline, uses the common everyday experience of fantasy. Normally, most of the creative power of the ability to imagine is lost in Walter Mitty type fantasy wanderings. Or worse, the mind conjures up ugly and depressing images which fuel melancholy, depression, and similar emotional disturbances. Yet through the guidance of the Holy Spirit, one can learn to use this same ability to erase old memories by replacing them with faith-empowered images. These images are deliberately constructed to fit into old memory sequences. There is a natural law in the universe which says that two things cannot occupy the same space at the same time. Using faith-imagination, the mind fills the emotional space occupied by a negative thought or memory with a new, more powerful, positive thought and image.

The purpose of this book is to introduce the reader to some methods of replacing negative memories with God-inspired reconstructions of those memories. My hope is that any who find benefit in these tools will pass them on. Here we have available a means of touching and transforming troubled hearts which is free of misleading impractical dogma or the pseudo-sophistication of academic psychology that by itself has been powerless to touch the minds of millions of people.

Through inner healing, the lonely can find release from their imprisonment. The depressed can find light to dispel impenetrable darkness. Those who feel unloved and rejected can find acceptance and the ability to give and receive this crowning emotion of love. The torment of guilt which seems indelible can be washed away. Until we have experienced this torment, or until we have been freed from it, we cannot appreciate on our own heart level the saying of Saint Paul that "the whole creation groans as if in the pangs of childbirth" to become more Christlike.[3] And when we have been freed from the tyrannies of repressed or long forgotten memories, we realize that creative thought is more powerful than negative thought because the creative flows from, into, and with this Christ-destined design of the universe.

1.

The Healing Power of
LOVE

There are at least two possible ways to define anything. Consider the following definitions of love.

¹love \'ləv\ n [ME, fr. OE *lufu*; akin to OHG *lupa* love, OE *lēof*
dear, L *lubēre*, *libēre* to please] 1 a : affection based on admiration
or benevolence b : an assurance of love 2 a : warm attachment,
enthusiasm, or devotion ⟨~ of the sea⟩ b : the object of such attachment or devotion 3 a : unselfish concern that freely accepts
another in loyalty and seeks his good: (1) : the fatherly concern of
God for man (2) : brotherly concern for others' b : man's adora-
tion of God 4 a : the attraction based on sexual desire : the
affection and tenderness felt by lovers b : a god or personification
of love c : an amorous episode : LOVE AFFAIR d : the sexual embrace : COPULATION 5 : a beloved person : DARLING 6 : a score
of zero in tennis 7 cap, *Christian Science* : GOD
²love *vt* 1 : to hold dear : CHERISH 2 a : to feel a lover's passion,
devotion, or tenderness for b : CARESS 3 : to like or desire
actively : take pleasure in ⟨*loved* to play the violin⟩ 4 : to thrive in
⟨the rose ~s sunlight⟩ ~ *vi* : to feel affection or experience desire

The Holy Spirit defined love in this way:

"And when they came to the place which is called The Skull, there they crucified him, and the criminals, one on the right and one on the left. And Jesus said, 'Father, forgive them; for they know not what they do.'"[1]

The first definition is purely intellectual. The second is embodied, world-changing and life-transforming.

Somewhere between that dictionary definition and Christ's divine definition we are constantly writing our own.

Each response we have to another person, even though it may not be verbalized, is a "definition" of love. It may be poorly stated and may even be ignored, but it is still our own. And often it is at variance with our verbalized expression. No matter what we say our definition of love is, the way we actually act and respond is our true definition. For whatever definition of love our heart chooses to embrace will determine the quality of love we manifest in our relationships. The better that heart definition, the better our lives will be.

A NEGATIVE DEFINITION OF LOVE

I knew a woman whose mother was a prostitute and whose father deserted the family shortly after Maria was born. After spending several hours in the home of a loving couple, Maria told them, "It disturbs me to spend much time in your home. I don't really know what 'love' is, but the closest thing that I have ever seen to what other people call 'love' I find here. I don't know why it always frightens me so. I can only take so much and then I want to run away. When I come here, I get the feeling you think I'm good and that makes me feel so hypocritical because I know how bad I really am."

"Maria," said the husband, "possibly you feel as you do because we love you so much. And you dislike yourself so much that you don't believe you deserve our love. It could be that this is why you feel uncomfortable in our home." He was right. To Maria, love was something related to sex, to being used or getting something from someone. The unconditional, generous love of this Christian couple confused her. Until her childhood, heart definition of love conditioned by her parents changed, she could neither receive love nor give it.

Nothing is more important to a newborn baby than feeling the warmth of love: the touch of loving hands on its tiny body, strong arms holding it close, the warmth of feeding at a waiting breast, and hearing the beat of the mother's heart, tears and laughter of a happy father and a joyous mother sharing this tiny miracle of God. A child's definition of love begins during these early, formative months, even though the child cannot voice it.

During Maria's infancy, the most important people in her life, her father and mother, began to desecrate a relationship which should have been a source of love and security.

This is why Maria could know nothing of an authentic definition of love. In her young years she might have described love as merely "the undependable sensual emotion which draws a man and woman together, causing birth, and then turns ugly, producing a feeling of being unwanted and unattractive."

No amount of intellectualizing, lecturing, or teaching could have helped this woman. Maria confessed that she had hated her own baby which had been born out of wedlock. And why not? Why should she not follow her parents' example and hate her own child? Why should not the cursed pattern be repeated unto the third and fourth generation, as the Law of Moses predicts,[2] or until she or one of her descendants experiences what the New Testament calls "the renewing of your minds"?[3]

Maria, as with each of us, is the inevitable product of her past. Our today is an accumulative expression of our yesterdays. All have been faithfully recorded in the memory bank in our deep mind. I would paraphrase Tennyson's statement, "I am a part of all that I have met," to say, "All that I have met on the level of my heart is a part of me."

The unhappy memories of being born unwanted or unloved had handicapped Maria and had conditioned her to live as an emotional invalid until the Spirit of God reconstructed her definition. Many people today are similarly handicapped until inner healing sets them free from the tyrannical claims of cruel memories, releasing them to live fuller and freer lives.

STEPS TOWARD A POSITIVE DEFINITION

The first step in Maria's inner healing occurred when she became a part of a loving relationship she could trust and accept. From there she has begun to learn what all who are unwanted at birth must discover: that they are greatly loved and accepted in God's family. This will be an ongoing process for Maria as she evolves toward the ultimate definition.

Inner healing is an essential part of this emotional and spiritual reconstruction.

Many who have had a living encounter with Christ question why areas of their inner emotional life are still resistant to love. Dedicated Christians are frequently unable to respond lovingly to people because, while they have experienced the elevating love of the Holy Spirit, they have limited knowledge of the meaning of love found in human relationships. They find it difficult to give or receive such love.

Maria's inability to understand love was due to a hateful relationship during childhood. Many of us, however, suffer from more subtle causes than the brutality and callous treatment she experienced. More frequently, circumstances and the mistakes of sincere and good parents leave a child confused about the nature and expression of love. Many children suffer from what might be called an emotional deficiency disease. They are not given enough love, enough of a sense of personal beauty and self-worth to allow them to reach their potential as human beings. They received as much love as their parents were capable of giving, but that frequently proves to be inadequate.

How Can Love Deficiency Be Healed?

Inner healing addresses itself to this misfortune, and faith-imagination is a primary tool. The God-given capacity to reconstruct the hate-perverted or love-starved past through creative imagination is a powerful means available to everyone.

To imagine, simply stated, is to "image-in." We create, or remember, an image and concentrate upon that picture until it registers upon our feelings. It is as though we are projecting camera slides on a screen in our heart. Our imagination may be fuzzy and out of focus, or it may be sharply focused.

5

Vivid imagination, or the clear focus of images in our heart, is a significant force in the reconstruction of our emotional past.

When the element of faith is added, it is as though Jesus becomes the projectionist. At this point the great mystery of his healing of our emotions begins. When Jesus is added to the image-creating process, his healing power is released—not only into the image which is changed, but into the emotions which have been damaged. This process defies logical analysis, but it is repeatedly confirmed by experience. I have seen hundreds of lives changed by this Christ-inspired faith-imagination. It is one of the most effective tools for inner healing.

By faith we can create the picture of Jesus traveling back through time to our childhood. It is nothing less than awesome to watch a person imagine Jesus walking with them into their painful past, and seeing them experience an actual transformation of negative emotion produced by loveless memories. Jesus is described in the Gospels as the one who "will not break a bruised reed."[4] Nowhere is that more evident than in inner healing. We can ask Jesus to go back through time to where we have been bruised. There he applies his love to the damaged emotions. Those who have never tried inner healing may not understand how a past event can be reconstructed and healed. To vividly imagine a past event is to relive it in the present. In much the same way that the past can be relived, the Spirit of God can re-create.

The realm of the Spirit is timeless. Every yesterday and every tomorrow is "today" to God. This may be a new truth to some because we live in the illusion that time is absolute. But even science has proved that absolute time is an illusion. Einstein proved that at the speed of light time ceases to exist. Jesus said, "I am the light of the world,"[5] and, in his Spirit, time dissolves into an eternal "now."

Jesus is the Lord of time, and this makes him the Lord of our past. Such Scriptures as, "Beloved, be not ignorant of this one thing, that one day is with the Lord as a thousand years, and a thousand years as one day,"[6] express this truth.

Because Jesus can bring his timeless presence into what we call "the past," he can bring the re-creative power of God to bear upon events that have already transpired. He promises to hear our prayer and answer before we even ask.[7] Jesus said that he was a part of the historical past in the present: "Before Abraham was, I am."[8] Therefore, we can believe that he can travel back with us through our short history. He can heal painful emotions by bringing his presence into the events formed by imperfect relationships. There, with infinite compassion, he heals and strengthens our bruised spirits and hurting hearts. The unique capacity of the mind of Christ is to allow maturity to evolve by providing the foundation of a healed past.

HOW TO EXPERIENCE JESUS' HEALING

This was the experience of Betty Terra. She could never remember feeling her daddy's arms around her. It was impossible for her to draw on any adequate experience of a mother's love. She could only recall hurting and wanting someone to love her.

As a child she often cried herself to sleep. When she reached her teenage years, the longing for someone to share her thoughts and needs became obsessive. Eventually, these longings turned inward and were replaced by self-hatred and condemnation for being weak and a crybaby.

As the pain was repressed and misdirected, Betty began to suffer psychosomatically. Frequently, she was physically ill. Then as her emotional structure disintegrated, she was in and out of mental hospitals. Tranquilizers dulled her pain. Shock therapy dulled her memory. But these steps are palliatives. They never heal. And after a period of temporary relief, feelings of hopeless despair would inundate her again. Her condition worsened until her arms and legs became numb and she had difficulty breathing. Periodically she would black out.

The next step in her emotional deterioration was withdrawal from her friends and their consequent rejection of her. Feeling totally abandoned, she attempted to take her life. Her attempt failed, but she spent long weeks in the hospital recovering from self-inflicted knife wounds.

When Betty was brought to an inner-healing workshop, she heard the unsophisticated but important message: God loved her; Jesus Christ cared for her. She panicked and tried to block out what she was hearing. What to a normal person would have been words of comfort and hope attacked her mind like sharp knives: "Jesus loves you! Jesus wants you to be whole. He wants to walk back through your life, into every painful experience you've ever had and remove the sting. He wants to remove the guilts within your life." Betty felt powerless to reach out to receive such love. She couldn't stand the thought of being rejected one more time.

But as the guided meditation continued, Betty

suddenly saw in her imagination Jesus standing before her. His arms went around her and he was saying he loved her. Such a mystical moment is not open to critical analysis. These spiritual dimensions lie far above the rational faculties.

At this point, Betty recounted to me later, her feelings of self-hatred began to emerge. But as they did, Jesus whispered, "It's okay, Betty. You're okay."

Betty continued, "Then the memory of taking the knife into my hand and gouging my flesh flashed before me. I saw Jesus reach over and take the knife out of my hand, touch my wound, and stop the flow of blood. I realized in that moment that the physical pain I had brought on myself was for the purpose of releasing my own emotional pain. A person can only hurt so much." This insight is psychologically right on target. Most psychosomatic conditions are the product of transferring the emotional load from the mind to the body, because the mind can stand only so much pain.

"Then, as I faced the meaning of my act, Jesus took me into his arms again. My mind flashed back to my childhood. I was a little girl being held in Daddy's arms. All of the emptiness, all the loneliness seemed to be wiped away and I was filled with warmth."

After this experience, Betty sought Christian counseling and companionship. She has begun her journey into emotional and spiritual healing. Her capacity to experience the love of Christ gradually has increased as she has yielded her imagination to the Holy Spirit and has allowed the great physician to continue the process of healing her past. Her story is not over. But it has a new beginning. She has been emotionally as well as physically born again!

How the Subconscious Controls

Psychology teaches us how the human mind functions and affects our lives. One assumption of this science is that the mind operates on at least two levels: the conscious and the subconscious.[9] Our conscious mind functions on the rational, cognitive level, recording impressions from the five senses: seeing, hearing, smelling, tasting, and touching. Our subconscious mind records *all* of the events we experience on the conscious level as well as many which we cannot remember. Those hidden from the conscious mind still influence conscious judgment. They unconsciously color and direct our thinking.

The conscious mind appears to be the most determinative level of decision making. But it is constantly influenced in that process by a flow of impressions from our feeling level. The subconscious is the great submerged area which stores these feelings and conditions our viewpoints. Our subconscious mind records likes and dislikes, training and lack of training, loves and hates, joys and sorrows—all happy and unhappy experiences. If we begin to understand that every pain we have ever had is subconsciously recorded, we cannot ignore the importance of these memories and the necessity of reconstructing the negative ones. It is to this storehouse of impressions that Jesus refers when he mentions "the heart of man." "For a man's words flow out of what fills his heart. A good man draws good things from his store of goodness; a bad man draws bad things from his store of badness."[10]

The period of most rapid learning in our lives is from birth to two years. Most authorities in the field of child development believe that before a child is of school age, most of his basic emotional patterns already have been formed.

Our subconscious memory, a mental computer, records everything. It forgets nothing. The only means we have of revising this emotional record is by the re-creative work of the Holy Spirit. And often the Spirit must redo our earliest recollections.

INFLUENCES BEFORE BIRTH

It is difficult for us to think in terms of prenatal influence. But the Scripture, which describes the joy of John the Baptist while in his mother's womb, offers a tantalizing clue as to how deeply affected we can be before birth. When John's mother Elizabeth was greeted by Mary, the mother of Jesus, and heard that Mary was to give birth to the Savior of the world, the unborn John "leaped for joy" in Elizabeth's womb.[11] Conversely, there is a growing body of evidence in counseling which indicates that children can be emotionally scarred during the period of gestation. Dwell for a moment on the barrage of shocks experienced by the unborn child of the unwed mother. Consider the stream of negative emotions flowing through the mother's body to the child as she experiences the shame of confession to parents, the threat of abortion, the fear of exposure, the painful trauma of giving birth to an unwanted child. This can have an incalculably destructive effect on the emotions of the unborn infant.

Adopted children usually need Jesus to heal unremembered "memories" of being born unwanted. They must be given the experience of a Jesus who can supply the love the unhappy mother was unable to give. The parents of most adopted children do a great service in making up for the child's inadequate experience of love. But only Christ can go back with the child into the womb and fill in that void during the prenatal period.

Jane is a classic example of what can happen to heal the emotional damage done to an unborn infant. She was an illegitimate child, and at the age of eleven she ran away from home. Eventually she became a member of a motorcycle gang, similar to Hell's Angels, because in the gang she felt acceptance—something no one else had given her. The gang led her into crime, drugs, and prostitution. By the time she was thirteen she was a drug addict.

When I met her, Jane told me that her life was over. She was filled with self-loathing. But after several sessions of sharing, she began to experience a degree of inner healing and gain a sense of hope. She began to respond to love. But everyday responsibilities were still difficult for her to handle. Her painful memories were deeply buried, torturing her sensitive spirit. I asked her if we could allow Jesus to walk back with her to the time of conception. At first she brushed the suggestion off as nonsense. Later, more out of courtesy to me, she consented.

She was led through a guided meditation which began at the moment of her conception. Christ was asked to be present when a young man and woman consummated the act that was to give birth to Jane.

"Jesus," I prayed, "in this moment touch that young man and woman with your holy love. Purify each of them through your grace. Remove all lust, all impure thoughts, and establish this conception in perfect love. And at this moment of impregnation, touch this newly formed life, consecrate it through your divine love."

I explained to Jane why she was no accident, that God knew her before she was conceived in her mother's womb, and that there were no accidents in God's kingdom.[12] I assured her that there may be unholy sex acts but that conception is holy and pure, an act of God, and that her birth had been ordained by her heavenly Father, God. This understanding implemented further healing. It gave her the sense of self-respect necessary for continued inner growth. The sense of disgrace related to her conception and birth began to fade as she accepted the truth that her life was a divine intention rather than a biological accident.

EVOLVING PROCESS OF INNER HEALING

Since inner healing is a process, any experience which reaches back to the first moments of life should be considered foundational, not complete. Any healing realized in this first process may not relieve the guilt and pain caused by emotional damage experienced in later years. Subsequent negative experiences must be dealt with as each incident is exposed by the Holy Spirit. The healing of a broken leg may enable a person to walk, but it does not automatically take care of an arm that may be fractured in a later fall.

Jane's prenatal healing must be viewed as a beginning. Later emotional injuries were dealt with separately. Inner healing can be compared to a chain where each past emotional hurt is linked to every other. As one link of the chain of emotional pain is healed, it opens the way for the healing of the next link. Psychiatric guidance can unearth the weak links but only divine guidance can re-create and heal with Christ's touch. And it is an incredible experience to observe how precisely each link of pain emerges when the preceding one has been healed.

Jane's prenatal experience attracted many later painful experiences; she was so negative in attitude that her negativity invited frequent rejection. When the root problem was healed, others were not invited to reject. When she unconsciously anticipated love, she attracted the acceptance she had wanted and needed all her life.

A further benefit of Jane's healing was that she gradually became more honest in her relationships. It began to hurt her now to see how she had blamed others for her problems. She was learning a new definition of love: to care for others and to be emotionally honest.

Like Jane, we usually blame others when we feel hurt or angry. On the journey toward spiritual enlightenment our first responsibility is to will not to blame others. We must see that while we cannot control the conduct of others, we can eventually control our reactions to that conduct. We all can recall persons or experiences that have consistently triggered our anger. It is painful to realize that the problem actually lies within ourselves, that it is not the fault of our antagonist. When we finally become willing to accept the responsibility for our emotional reaction, we are on the high road to inner healing.

A man who frequently felt uncontrollable anger toward his wife told me that even when he didn't physically express his anger, he felt consumed with frustration and rage. In time, he came to see that one way to control his irrational feelings was to stop blaming her. One night his resolve was put to the test. There was a difference of opinion between them. Then, as so often happens, the reaction escalated to an ego warfare with heated words exploding into bitter personal denunciation. Each felt the other was being unfairly accusing. Finally, the wife touched the nerve in the husband which sent him into a paroxysm of bitterness: she accused him, falsely, of unfaithfulness. She had learned from previous experience that such an attack triggered rage in him. But he was determined not to blame her, so he retreated into silence, his arms folded across his chest—in vivid body language expressing the need to protect his emotions.

His unfamiliar reaction jolted her into a realization of her mistake. She immediately asked his forgiveness.

But he failed to respond. He sat frozen in inner conflict. He knew he must face himself, but he felt powerless to do so. She tried a further act of reconciliation. "Since you don't want me close to you," she said, "let me just massage your feet." With these words she got some lotion and began tenderly to rub his feet.

This act of love reached in and freed him to express the bitterness he felt. He flew into a tirade about her cruelty, about how jealous and unreasonable she was. The explosion seemed to blow the lid off a storehouse of resentment over maternal tyranny. As never before, it laid bare the snake pit of half-buried emotions seething within him. Angers surfaced from early childhood when he first began to experience an unhealthy relationship with his mother. She frequently attacked and blamed him for many innocent things. As a defenseless child, he could not escape. As an adult, this conditioning had poisoned most of his relationships with women and most especially the marital relationship.

As his rage burst to the surface he drew back his clenched fist and cried, "I'm so angry I'm going to drive my fist through that wall!" "Don't hit the wall," his wife cried. "You'll hurt yourself. Hit me."

Later, reflecting on his wife's unconditional, very tough love, the husband declared this to be the moment that set him free. "I dropped my clenched fist," he said, "and wept for an hour. Something I still don't completely understand was healed inside. I feel different toward women in general and my mother in particular because my wife came across that night with a truckload of love and tenderness."

It would be an unfruitful task to analyze such a healing moment. But one thing is clear: there was a sequence of events triggered by a man's will to stop blaming another. When he first made that resolve, he appeared to be far from the required breakthrough. But his will not to blame another provided the leverage needed to lift him to receive an experience of transforming love.

LEARNING TO AFFIRM LOVE

The incomparable biblical definition for God is "God is love."[13] And we live only to the degree that we are able to receive and give this love which is God. The task of inner healing is to open us to the infinite stream of Love in which we can live and move and have our being. We don't have to go out looking for it. It is as ever-present as the air we breathe. But our capacity to receive the Spirit of healing love is limited by our inner pain. That is part of the human dilemma—poverty in the midst of abundance. Our challenge is to grow in our capacity to receive that Love. But to realize that increase, our heart definition of Love must be upgraded. Whatever does this is the handmaid of inner healing. Every encounter with Christlike love, a love which, even though flawed, seeks to bear all things, believe all things, hope all things, endure all things,[14] is a catalyst for inner healing.

In the immortal song of love written by St. Paul, the qualities of this highest definition are made specific. In our quest to know and experience such a definition on the affective level of life, it is helpful to affirm these qualities to our inner child. It is valueless to scold ourselves when we don't measure up to them. In fact, it retards our capacity to appropriate a higher definition of Love. But to claim them as our own, as an act of faith, encourages our heart to absorb the richer expression of Love. It helps the easily intimidated inner child of the subconscious to live these virtues.

Here is the definition of highest love found in 1 Corinthians 13. It has been revised into a series of affirmations. A morning and evening review of them will prove most productive.

I am very patient and kind.
I am never jealous or envious.
I do not make excuses for myself.
I am never boastful or proud . . . I always have time to do the things that are needful for I know that with God all things are possible.

I am never haughty, or selfish, or rude.

I am successful, never operating under my own strength.

I do not demand my own way.

I am never irritable or touchy.

I am optimistic and confident under all circumstances.

I never hold grudges.

I am full of kindness.

I am never glad about injustice.

I always rejoice when truth wins out.

The goal of giving and receiving perfect love is a lofty one. But we need not be intimidated. Love is patient. We will know sustained satisfaction as we obey the biblical instruction, "Make love your aim."[15]

2.

The Healing Power of
FAITH

Several years ago my mother-in-law had a stroke. She fell out of the hospital bed, suffered a concussion and couldn't move. Attending physicians labeled her "totally and hopelessly paralyzed." When the doctor told my husband that she could not possibly live for more than three days he flew to her home to be by her side and to make funeral arrangements.

The day after we had received the news about my mother-in-law, I went to my small group meeting. They were all college students with whom I had been sharing some of the truths I had been learning. "I really have a need now," I told them. "We're going to have to put into practice the things I've been teaching you. I want to sit in this prayer circle and I want to be the intercessor. I want you to pray for my husband, and my father-in-law; one is losing his mother, the other his wife."

One of those students looked at me and asked, "Ruth, whom did you say to pray for?"

"For my father-in-law, and for my husband because he is an only child."

Another one continued, "Well, didn't you say it was your mother-in-law who was sick?"

"Yes," I said, "but her life is over now. I mean death has really set in."

One of the students said, "Ruth, I believe that you need prayer more than any of them."

They quoted some of the scriptures that I had taught them. But at that time I apparently didn't have the faith to believe that my mother-in-law would be healed. My mind was filled with mental pictures of her sickened condition. The students asked me to sit in a chair, then gathered around me. Because I didn't have the faith to believe, one young student prayed, "Jesus, give Ruth the faith to believe that all things are possible."

In a moment I was flooded with a supernatural presence. My whole attitude was changed, not only my mind, but my heart. When I said to them, "I believe," they began to pray for my mother-in-law's wholeness—for her complete healing. This, I know now, was God's response, the fulfillment of his promise to give his children the faith needed in the moment that they ask.

I had not mentioned to the students that my mother-in-law had been a semi-invalid for the past thirteen years before the stroke. If I had told them that, they might have prayed only for healing from the stroke. But they were inspired to pray for her total healing.

POSITIVE IMAGINATION

In my mind's eye, I began to see her whole, not as the doctors had described her. I visualized her happy, working around the house, enjoying life to the fullest.

Six days later, my husband called to report that not only was his mother still alive but she was showing signs of improvement. The doctors reported that her esophagus was no longer paralyzed. So, each day I would continue my spiritual homework. I would visualize her walking, singing, and happy.

By July, she could hear and move her lips a little.

In September, she had recovered sufficiently to go home. Still she had to be attended around the clock by special nurses.

By November, she had recovered enough to ride by motor car with her husband from Georgia to North Carolina to spend Thanksgiving with our family. And while she was with us we did our Christmas shopping together.

In January, she released her maid of thirteen years. She simply didn't need her any more. She was a new person, able to do her own driving, sewing, cooking—in fact, everything she had been able to do before she had become ill.

Two essential factors permitted this miracle to happen. First, the childlike faith of the students in the prayer group. They provided a community, a climate of vital faith. It seems clear that circumstances of great need require the faith of many people. There is a gigantic leap of power in collective faith. This principle is negatively expressed in the situation where Jesus could "not do many mighty works" because of the unbelief of the people of his hometown of Nazareth.[1] Even Jesus was hindered by the absence of a community of faith.

The second factor in my mother-in-law's healing was my healing. What those praying students did for me was provide a channel for God's grace to touch my doubt-ridden mind. My spirit had been injured by the dogmatic, faithless prognosis of sincere but spiritually imperceptive doctors. They were sure their patient could not live. And I accepted that verdict. It didn't dawn on me that they could be wrong. They had the training and the credentials. It all boils down to the sad fact that I believed in the word of the doctors more than the word of God. But the faith of those young people allowed God to heal my impaired spiritual vision. I began to see things as God saw them. And that is what faith is: seeing circumstances as God sees them—whole, beautiful, filled with his love.

DEFENSE MECHANISMS PREVENT HEALING

How many people are needlessly suffering because of a lack of faith? Life for them is one disaster after another waiting to happen. They fear sickness, tragedy, war, privation and hosts of other plagues. In their view, God is not in control, and that means they are a victim in life waiting to be victimized. It is not surprising that they often receive what they expect! Ironically, their fears create a climate which assures them the misfortune they fear.

For many seeking deeper inner healing and faith, an important question is: what do I fear? Am I asking for it—am I asking life to fulfill my fears? But very often we cannot answer such questions because we are not in touch with our feelings.

For the first twenty-nine years of my life I felt almost no emotional pain. But later, when many of the repressed hurts of my past were exposed, I began to feel intense inner pain. The reason I did not see my hurts earlier is that unconsciously I would not allow myself to look.

Each of us has developed a defense mechanism which keeps us from looking at our weak self-image. But the problem with this mental attitude is that when our insecurity compels us to pull up our draw-bridge, it not only keeps our enemies out, but it also denies entrance to our friends, and keeps out of our life love, trust, and sharing, to name only a few. When we are insecure, we find it difficult to establish rewarding relationships; nor can we exercise faith in those relationships when we are ruled by our fears. Our castle becomes our dungeon.

It seems, then, that what often needs to be healed are not only the hurts of our past but also the defenses we put up to protect ourselves because of those hurts. There is an instinctive, protective mechanism in human nature which, when unaided by God, builds scar tissue on our emotions. Just as with physical scar tissue, what is meant to protect makes us less sensitive. We become less in touch with our feelings. It usually takes surgery to eliminate the insensitivity. And often the only scalpel sharp enough to remove this ugly, protective layer is pain. When that pain is experienced, it is important to have friends nearby with faith in Jesus' love and healing power. In other words, if a person is seeking deep inner healing it should be done in a context of the loving, nurturing fellowship of those who care.

FEAR—THE OPPOSITE OF FAITH

When our protective faculties are highly developed, and inner stress has no way of being ventilated or of healing, we run the risk of emotional breakdown. The reason is we are not sufficiently in touch with our feelings of depression, exhaustion, and guilt, and the overload of unrelieved stress expresses itself in emotional collapse.

For example, if we have developed a fear of being in groups, we will avoid situations where people are present in large numbers. At first we may avoid going to the theater, or sports events. By avoiding crowds, our protective actions have been reinforced by the absence of fear. Consequently, we become more reclusive. We may then avoid riding the bus, or going out to dinner even with our families. Eventually, the pattern of avoiding people will become so pronounced that we can no longer function with any semblance of normalcy. We then become incapable of caring for our families because we fear going to the grocery store, or taking our children to the doctor or dentist. We become victimized by the very pattern which was developed to protect us.

What is obviously true in the radical case of the recluse, is just as true of more normal persons whose less malignant fears cause them to deny themselves the right to relate to others in love and trust.

One way to deal with our fears is not to fight them directly. We must face them, but to attack them head-on can be traumatic. To concentrate upon a fear may intensify it and cause us to fear the fear. An alternative solution is to root out the original cause. But this discovery frequently comes after successive experiences of lifting off layer upon layer of protective material.

The recluse may have a child whom she loves. And as she watches her condition produce a functional deterioration in the child, her maternal instincts are aroused and the decay is more than she can bear. So she begins to look for help. She goes to a prayer group about which she has heard. She is panic-stricken in the group, but the fear for her daughter overshadows her personal fears, and the first step beyond herself is taken. At the meeting she can't ask for personal help but she does ask the group to pray for her daughter. That is one further step toward her healing. She has reached out for help. And if the group is caring and warm, the foundation is laid for further steps.

The subsequent encounters with caring people will be filled with conduct unconsciously intended to test the water. The fear of being hurt still exists. She may become morose or have a fit of temper in the meeting or with one of the group members privately. A positive, understanding reaction is essential for her continued growth. In this context, one can see why judgment of another's conduct is superficial, inappropriate and damaging. Displays of temper or moodiness should evoke sympathy and helpful understanding, rather than criticism or correction.

When love finally cuts away the protective callouses, the actual cause is revealed and healed.

A more common fear is rooted in the feeling that if anyone should find out what we are really like they would reject us. This insecurity causes us to live in a constant state of tension. If we are controlled by this anxiety, we have abandoned our God-given privilege of being our unique self—warts and all.

How Fear May Be Healed

One of the ways of defeating this fear is to discover the unfailing, constant love and acceptance of Jesus Christ. When we learn that Jesus knows everything we have said, felt or done, and loves us unconditionally, the cold grip of fear of rejection is broken. It often takes an experience of unconditional love from another person to open the way to the experience of Christ's love. Jesus is the foundation of all answers to every problem. He is the conqueror of every fear in life. To the degree that we can believe with our minds and hearts that we are loved by Jesus we will be free of fear.

We do not fear poverty if we have faith in God's provision. We do not fear punishment for misdeeds when we believe God loves us. We do not fear being ourselves with others when we know we are totally accepted by God just as we are. He died for us while we were still sinners to let us know how much we are loved. And that same love seeks to bring us the gift of inner healing any time we are ready.

Timetable for Healing

The inner healing process usually requires many months, even years. The reasons for this are several. Who could bear to look at all our buried heartaches at once? Because this pain would be intolerable, the Spirit usually surfaces them one at a time. We are able to face one note or one bar of discordant music, and as this segment is brought into harmony, we are being prepared for the next.

Another reason is that it takes time to establish new patterns of behavior after the old memories are eliminated. New patterns of thought are gradually translated into established patterns of conduct in much the same way that we learn to walk. The process begins first as a halting self-conscious effort, and only after repeated returns to this new experience does it become an automatic creative experience.

A woman came for counseling who had just attempted suicide. She said that total despair arose from her husband's unfaithfulness. What she didn't realize was that her extreme reaction to the infidelity was founded in the death of her father when she was two years old. His death had left her with deep, largely repressed, feelings of male rejection. Her husband's conduct had confirmed her fear of being deserted by men.

During counseling the woman was able to see and deal with this fear. Through the miracle of the timeless ministry of Jesus, she went back to her father's death. By faith-imagination she was a little girl of two as she sat beside me, looking at her daddy in the casket. But Jesus, who stood beside her, touched her father as he did the widow's son whom he resurrected in the city of Nain centuries before. The father rose from the casket and took his little daughter in his arms—she had her daddy again.

That was the great and glorious beginning. In the new confidence that all men are not deserters, a new relationship could now begin with her husband. In her daily encounters she faces flickers of the once-devastating pain, but she now has the faith to experience love and forgiveness. As she learns to love and forgive him, strength and substance are being added to her new positive image of the male. All of this is taking time.

There is also a negative reason for the slow progress

in inner healing. We often want just enough healing to bring relief to our suffering. Then a complacency sets in. The God who will not invade our free will simply waits for a further crisis to prepare us for more exposure and healing. God will win in his goal to perfect us. Life is on his side and will reveal our ignored emotional flaws, and we will be healed as we yield to God's love.

The pattern in healing often resembles the peeling of an onion. But usually the Spirit peels our "onion" from the inside out. An early traumatic memory rises to the consciousness, and when it is removed, another one surfaces. As we focus in on more recent hurts, generally we can assume that the process of healing a particular pain is nearly over—but not always. Now we are ready to deal with a deeply repressed memory which earlier we could not handle. No matter—we must be patient. We must let the Spirit heal us in his way and according to his timetable.

How long will the healing process take? Much depends upon how much we have repressed, and how thick our emotional defenses are. Sometimes the psychic walls which human instinct erects around a terrible childhood pain, pain that it could not endure, are amazingly thick. The greater the pain, the thicker the wall. The thicker the wall, the more time God's healing may take.

When deeply repressed feelings such as fear, anger, sexual feelings, or intense traumatic memories are involved, it is sometimes good that we have barriers to guard us, to protect us from the onslaught of the implicit emotion. When this is the case, we need to experience growth on a conscious level in order to mature enough to deal with awareness of these problem areas.

God works within the natural order he has established. "First the blade, then the ear, after that the full corn in the ear."[2] Most normal growth is slow and continuous. There must be this same continuity in our emotional growth. We don't suddenly achieve instant perfection. We unfold like the grain.

How Do We Get Faith?

If our negative attitudes hinder our believing that God can begin to heal us, our first prayer should be that we be given his gift of faith.

Faith is not something that we can create at will. We must depend on the Spirit to supply adequate faith to meet the situation. Faith is one of the gifts of the Spirit described in 1 Corinthians 12. God in his love knows that we need more of this priceless quality than we can muster, and so he provides it as a gift to any who ask. We are the beloved children of God, and he delights to lavish such gifts on us. All we need to do is reach out and accept what he offers.

But this raises the frequently asked question, "How do we know it is God's will that a person be healed?" We know because God is love. And love always wills wholeness, happiness, and blessings for the object of its expression. I think that Leslie Weatherhead in his book *The Will of God* has made an enlightening distinction between what he terms the "perfect will of God" and the "circumstantial will of God."

To illustrate, he recalls a conversation with a missionary in India. The missionary's little son had just died of diphtheria. "I accept my son's death," he said to Weatherhead, "because it was the will of God."

29

"What do you mean, 'the will of God'?" said Weatherhead. The baby daughter of the man was lying near them in a crib under mosquito netting. "What if I took a cotton swab, dipped it in diphtheria culture and pressed it into your daughter's mouth? What would you do to me?"

"I suppose I'd want to kill you, like I'd kill a mad dog!" the man exclaimed.

"Then," concluded Weatherhead, "don't blame God for your son's death. Blame man's greed and selfishness, his willingness to spend fortunes on war and relatively nothing on medical research. Blame it on man's ignorance, on open sewage. But don't blame it on God."

Then Weatherhead states the truth that the perfect will of God is that sickness be replaced with health in everyone. But human factors such as faithlessness, carelessness, and sloth can block this perfect will. So, God's circumstantial will is that the condition remain unhealed. Under the circumstances God cannot heal. But given man's faith and faithfulness, healing would be realized.

Finally, there is no evidence in the Gospels that anyone who came to Jesus for healing did not receive it. Jesus never said concerning healing, "If it is God's will . . ." Obviously he assumed that it was.

How Do We Maintain Faith?

Therefore let us assume that faith is our rightful gift. The pressing question then becomes, "How can I maintain a strong faith? At times my faith seems so weak." The answer is given in Romans 10:17: "So faith comes from hearing, and hearing by the word of Christ."[3] We need to hear and contemplate the word of God. We should memorize many of God's promises. Most of our beloved "psalms and hymns and spiritual songs" memorized and sung through the day are a rich source of faith inspiration. When held in our memory, we can call on them in crisis and feed on them daily.

What we often forget and what many who do not believe in the Bible cannot begin to perceive is that the Bible proclaims the experience of those who have trusted God throughout the ages. By reading the story of their faith, we can enrich ours immeasurably. Our faith must be in God. Healing faith can never be in people, in doctors, medical science, or even prayer groups, or spiritual leaders. Our faith has to be centered in the person of Jesus Christ. He is the Source. He has urged us to ask that we might receive.[4] And if we believe, we will. The more deeply we believe, the more we will ask and receive. But that means we must hope. And hope means waiting expectantly, claiming and ceaselessly praising until we believe even more fully. Through hope we become saturated with the possibility, then the probability of the healing. Hope is the sustained sunlight which thaws the winter ice, so the healing waters of the Spirit may flow to the infirm.

VISUALIZING A MIRACLE

It is important to visualize a positive image in the situation confronted. When group imagination is negative, the first order of business is to bring it to an image of positive faith. Otherwise prayers are an exercise in futility, because the two forces conflict. The prayer is asking for God's help but the mental image held by the doubting expects no help.

At a recent ladies' church program, one of the women said, "Since our minister is in the hospital with a heart attack, why don't we take up a collection and buy him a pair of pajamas? The doctor says he will probably be there for another six weeks."

Everybody agreed the gift of pajamas was a good idea. As an afterthought, someone tentatively wondered, "Why don't we pray for him, too?"

They asked me to lead the prayer. But as we all bowed our heads, I suddenly realized I didn't know how to pray in this situation. "What are we going to ask for?" I asked them. "That the pajamas fit? Or, shall we ask that Jesus Christ, who is the same yesterday and today, heal that man completely—tonight— so that he can come home from the hospital and preach next Sunday?"

They looked as bewildered as I felt. I asked, "How many of you believe that Jesus heals today, and that he can heal your minister tonight? Let's be absolutely honest. Do you really believe it?"

Not one person could say yes. They admitted their lack of faith. That was an honesty which allowed us to deal with the negative image they were holding. In essence, they were confessing, "We see our minister sick in the hospital for several weeks." So first we prayed that God would lift our faith and help us see through his eyes.

As we prayed, the hearts of those women were changed. After a long, profound silence, I asked the question again. This time each one said, "Yes, I do believe. I believe Christ can heal him." Now there was a positive consensus. The image held by the women was one of their minister touched by the power of God and healed of the heart condition. We only have to believe long enough to voice a prayer, and it is done. If moments later our unbelief returns it does not lessen the power of the faith-filled petition. Once set in motion, the creative forces achieve their stated goal. The healing work may be reversed later by an outpouring of collective doubt. But the work first claimed by faith will be done.

In that creative instant, we all were in one accord as we prayed, "Lord Jesus, we believe that you are the same tonight as you were when you healed long ago. Touch this minister now, tonight in his hospital room. Make him whole."

And Jesus did. For the next two days my phone was ringing incessantly. The minister had made nothing less than a miraculous recovery. Two days later, he was released from the hospital, having missed only one Sunday service.

Five minutes after the prayer for his healing hardly a woman in that group believed that their minister would, in fact, be healed. But while they did believe, holding a positive image of him, they prayed. And he was healed.

COMPARISON OF TWO HEALINGS

There are significant differences between the two experiences of my mother-in-law's healing and the minister's. Some of them raise issues which deserve comment. While both group prayers resulted in complete physical healing of the prayer-target, the minister was back on his feet almost immediately while my mother-in-law took months to recover. There was a marked contrast in the perspective of the two groups. The young students had a more immediate faith and greater certainty about Christ's power to heal which seemingly should have created an immediate cure. But other factors, such as my mother-in-law's long conditioning to accept her illness and the grave certainty of all around her that she would momentarily be dead, had to be overcome. Greater power was needed to lift her gradually from the grave than was necessary to correct instantly the minister's condition.

For both groups, the end result was identical. There was a greater certainty that Christ, not the human diagnostician, is the ultimate authority in healing. Such experiences build great faith, and the result is that Christ becomes a deeper living reality to us. We are given greater belief in prayer. Since it is a personal experience, it is shared by the subconscious. That makes it far more vital in our ongoing attitudes toward life and God. Thus it plants the seeds for a fruitful future harvest of faith when later needs arise.

Predictably, the effect on the two patients healed was the most profound of all. Something had happened to the very cells of their bodies which made them know what once they only faintly believed. I don't think it is coincidence that one of the most noted ministers of healing was once healed. Oral Roberts rose from a deathbed, a victim of terminal tuberculosis, to challenge the world to "expect a miracle." His message was believable because he believed it. He more than believed, he knew. His healed lungs, the fact he was still alive, witnessed to him every moment of every day that Jesus Christ is the great physician. Academic discussion to the contrary can be silly or sacrilegious. He knows in each fiber of his body that Jesus heals.

THE HEALING OF EMOTIONS

I found myself in the ministry of inner healing because I had experienced the compassionate touch of
Christ on my shattered heart. I saw him take carefully, gently, gradually my hopelessly angry, frightened, immature little girl self, living in the body of
a young woman, and help that inner child of the
past put the broken pieces together and make life
worth living. Of course I believe that God can heal
sick emotions. Of course I know that Christ can re-
create our emotional and spiritual world. He did it
for me. And it is no secret, therefore, why I am
determined to minister to the emotionally troubled.
I am a member of that fellowship of Christ's suffering.[5]

It is not enough, however, simply to recall our
hurtful or painful experiences. Mere recollection does
not bring healing. It is only when we experience
the love of Jesus touching the traumatic emotion
caused by those hurtful experiences that we are
healed. This is an act made possible only through
faith. St. Paul explains that Christ in his love will
reach deep within the human heart and remove the
sting.[6] The reference to a bee sting is appropriate.
Because even after the stinger is removed the pain
remains. It takes as much faith to overcome the pain
as it did the original sting.

A letter I received from a woman I had met at
a conference illustrates this fact. "For some weeks
past," she wrote, "I have been troubled with a silly
bit of a cough which comes on every morning, and
often keeps me awake at nights. (This has recurred
at times for many years, whenever I have had a
cold.)

"My sister and I have been sharing a room this week, and last night she asked me whether I had asked for my cough to be healed in the Blessing Service. I said, 'No, I hadn't thought of it, and hadn't asked for anything actually.' She asked if I would mind if she prayed for it. I accepted gladly, so she placed her hand on this spot on my chest, and then just prayed a little prayer about it.

"Well, during the night things were about as usual, but then as it was just beginning to get light this morning, I wakened with a childhood memory. Now when you had been talking about deep inner healing the other evening, I had thought to myself that I didn't have any need for that sort of thing, having enjoyed a very happy childhood. . . . But this morning I wakened with this old memory in my mind. I would have been about six at the time, I suppose, and had been sent by my mother to get something from a druggist. I had to wait quite a time to be served, and while waiting, I read a notice on the wall. I can't be sure of the wording, but it was to the effect, 'Don't cough. Every time you cough you damage your lungs. Every time you damage your lungs, it brings you one step nearer consumption!' Now for some unknown reason, consumption was the one thing I really feared. I wondered, could this be the cause of this cough?

"So, I decided to do as you told us, and I invited Jesus to go back with me in time and enter that druggist's shop. But I couldn't think of any positive helpful notice to put up in exchange for that one on the wall! Presently it seemed as if he said to me: 'Well, suppose you let me use my little scalpel of love, and just scoop out that little lump that keeps bothering you, and then you'll never need to cough again unless you want to.' I thought that would be lovely, so he said, 'I'll do it while you sleep,' then added, '. . . and if you find you still manage a few coughs, remember it's just a ding-dong!'

"I must explain that before going to sleep, I had been reading one of Corrie Ten Boom's books, *Tramp for the Lord*, in which Chapter 32 was entitled 'Ding-Dong.' It was the story of a woman who had been delivered from evil thoughts and had confessed to Corrie that sometimes these thoughts still bothered her, and she was so afraid it meant that Satan was getting hold of her again. Corrie reassured her by saying that it was a bit like the big bell in the church belfry. Satan no longer had hold of the rope, but after the bell rope had been let go it still did a few 'ding-dongs' on its own as it slowed down, and Satan was trying to frighten her into believing he was still there!

"So, every time I've coughed today I've told myself it's just a ding-dong and I haven't had to take any notice of the old symptoms, since Jesus has healed me."

Faith frequently must deal with emotional "ding-dongs." If we repossess recurring weaknesses and infirmity we affirm them; we give them new substance. If we claim healing and wholeness we reinforce that work. Our will to believe in wholeness determines our ability to remain whole. A positive attitude and declaration brings a positive result, but a negative confession will bring a negative result. The person who, after inner healing, declares, "I am healed of my past hurts and wounds," will maintain the continuing process of healing. But the same person will lose much of the healing power if he negates his experience by saying, "I was prayed for, but I don't feel any better." We must never rely upon our feelings. Sustained faith is the highway to wholeness.

FAITH RATHER THAN FEELINGS

Many people ask me if I constantly walk in the joy of God's Spirit. I tell them that with growing consistency I feel that joy, but there are periods when I feel a desperate lack of joy. At one particular point in my growth I experienced a frightening absence of positive feeling. I had never felt such a void of love, of caring, of joy. In this valley of the shadow of dead emotions, I learned the importance of walking by faith. The "pioneer and perfecter of our faith," Jesus, shows us the way.[7] He struggled with human feelings of despair and fear in the Garden of Gethsemane. And it was only by raw faith that he moved on to total triumph for us.

When I first came to know Christ, I knew ecstasy. It was like a honeymoon for months. But the day came when suddenly it seemed as though I had been abandoned by Christ. My human conditioning led me to fear that God had left me. I worried that I had lost all the spiritual blessing I once had. As our loving Father, God sometimes allows us to experience overwhelming feelings in the beginning, when we need it. But as we begin to mature, he wisely must wean us from euphoria. He must teach each of us to walk by faith rather than living upon enjoyable but unreliable feelings. He knows that tests increase the strength of our faith. He allows us to see the superiority of faith over feelings. And *then* he restores the feelings. So, as we seek first the kingdom of God which is the kingdom of faith, all the feelings are added unto us.

During the two years when I experienced no conscious sense of the love or glory of God, I decided that I should stop speaking to groups. I regarded it as hypocritical to be telling of the healing love of God when I was so sick of myself and felt no love from him or for him. Then he graciously touched my heart. I began to realize that I was entering a new dimension of spiritual growth. I was being taught to walk by faith. With that insight, I made a new commitment:

"Lord, if I never feel your presence again, if I never feel your love any more, if I never feel that I want to help anybody, if I never want to speak for you again, I commit myself to walk by faith in obedience to your word. I commit myself to Jesus Christ without feeling."

With that prayer of faith, a quiet peace came. No longer did it matter what I felt. I believed God, not my feelings. Something quite unexpected happened. I was not instantly filled with a sense of God's presence, but there was a marked increase of spiritual power in my life. Clearly God was not dependent on my feelings at all! But he was dependent on my faith.

By releasing the need to feel exuberant or joyous, I experienced a new freedom. I knew that I didn't need to work up feelings. If positive feelings come, that is fine. I accept them as added blessings from God. And I'm deeply grateful for those long periods when I am filled with love for him and for others. However, if the feelings stop, I know that he is the same as always and can assume that I am in another learning period. So, I continue to minister, to pray, to speak for him. And no matter what my state of feelings may be, no matter what old negative emotional ghosts start to haunt me, I am assured deep within my spirit by faith that they will pass and that I have the companionship and love of Jesus always.

3.

The Healing Power of
SURRENDER

To a society which idolizes self-sufficiency and independence, the idea of surrendering to God meets great resistance. The word *surrender* evokes images of a vanquished foe humiliated in defeat. The idea of spiritual surrender calls up in the minds of most of us an image of God as an almighty tyrant who demands our subjugation.

In reality, surrender to God is the act of yielding self-destructive patterns to him, loosing our death-grip on the poison vials of hate, fear, resentment, and jealousy. Surrender is, positively stated, the will to find the kingdom of God within. Since the kingdom of God is a state of consciousness where one is creative, motivated by love which produces a state of joy, it is strange that we cling to the refuse of our self-will. But we are all like St. Augustine before his conversion who said that the sin he knew was more to be desired than the joy he did not know. We are afraid of the unknown, and often this is what causes us to resist surrender to God.

To tell a frightened nonswimmer, "Relax, you really can float, you don't need to thrash and kick and try to stay afloat," would be cruel. A demonstration of how to float would be more appropriate than verbal instruction. Similarly, to tell one who has never surrendered any area of their life to God, "Just surrender; beneath you are 'the everlasting arms.' "[1] could result in a spiritual drowning. In order to overcome fear, we need to be shown how to surrender, and to see a demonstration of the healing which can result.

The Creative Moment of Despair

Some people are already broken in spirit. They find it easier to relinquish control of their lives to God. There are also the childlike who need no experience of being broken. They simply open their spirits to God's will because they know it is the only path to take. The persons who most resist surrender to God are the spiritual rebels, the emotional addicts who have already surrendered their life to other gods: alcohol, sensuality, drugs, self-esteem, wealth, fame and power. To such slaves of selfishness, there must come the moment of total despair which will lead them to the point of creative surrender.

The need for such surrender was dramatically illustrated in the life of Bob, a corporation executive. He was vice president of one of the major corporations in America—and an alcoholic. His addiction began to take its toll, and his wife found the situation unbearable. In despair she sought the assistance of

John, her minister. After a lengthy phone conversation she concluded the description of her husband's drinking and gambling problem with the request, "If you ever get a chance to speak with him, please do it. We can't go on much longer like this."

Several days later Bob stopped by the minister's office asking for a recommendation for his son to be sent to an Eastern prep school. When they had finished their conversation, the minister, who was spiritually sensitive and psychologically knowledgeable, asked as matter-of-factly as he could, "By the way, Bob, how are things going with you?"

Bob stiffened and replied curtly, "What do you mean? Has someone said something?"

John smiled and responded, "I'm interested in every person that comes into this office."

"Well, I am having a little trouble with too much drinking, but I can handle it."

The moment Bob said, "I can handle it," John knew that his kindest response would be to say no more to Bob but to pray that the Spirit would quickly allow the emotional pain to surface, to be brought violently, if need be, to Bob's attention. This, he knew, would be necessary before the man would seek help. Those events usually are waiting just around the corner for the stubbornly resistant person.

A few days later, in tears, Bob's wife called the pastor. Her husband had mortgaged the home, and had lost everything in a wild spree of gambling and drinking. She pleaded with John to try to talk to Bob one more time. Against his better judgment, he agreed to do so.

Arriving at a palatial mansion, he was ushered into the living room by a butler. There Bob met him with icy hostility and resistance to any advice.

This incident confirmed in John's mind that basic rule of not offering a person help until the person asks for it. He would not involve himself until Bob had reached the point of surrender.

A month later, the necessary disaster struck. Another near-hysterical phone call from Bob's wife informed John that her husband had gone on a weekend binge. Early Monday morning, while in a drunken stupor, he had somehow stumbled into his suite of offices, disrobed, and fallen naked to the floor of the reception room of the outer office. When one of his secretaries found him, she ran for one of the other executives in the company. An emergency meeting of the board was called and Bob was summarily dismissed.

Bob's wife, at this point, felt the pressure of self-preservation. She had to save his livelihood, as well as to help him find sobriety. She pleaded with their pastor to intercede by speaking on Bob's behalf to the company president. John made it clear that although the president of the corporation was a friend and member of his congregation, he would not intercede unless Bob was willing to seek the help of God and the assistance of Alcoholics Anonymous.

Going to the hospital where Bob had been admitted, he found the once sophisticated businessman cowering under the sheet, crying like a frightened child.

"Bob, are you willing to talk now?" John asked.

"Anything, John. I'll do anything," he wept.

The minister then told him that his only hope was to seek the power of God to free him from the destructive power of alcoholism. Through surrender to Christ, sobriety was possible. Christ's healing power, he promised, would make him a new man if only he would abandon himself to Christ. And Bob surrendered to God.

From that day on, Bob never touched alcohol. He was reinstated as vice president of the corporation and became an active member of Alcoholics Anonymous.

Six years later, Bob retired honorably from the company. Since then, on the first Sunday of every November, the anniversary of the tragic awakening weekend, Bob commemorates that day in the hospital room when he surrendered his life by being in the congregation where John is preaching. One year he even traveled to Toronto, Canada, to be with him. And always at the end of the service, the distinguished, white-haired man, with his wife beside him, shakes his minister's hand and says simply, "Thank you, John. Thank you." He has never missed that anniversary of his new life.

When Bob said, "I'll do anything," this was a form of surrender. What formerly was characterized as loss, what began as the threat of losing his freedom, became the key to the new experience of liberation. Bob in his ignorance had become enslaved to emotions that were destroying him.

Our habits and attitudes may not be as antisocial as Bob's, but they can be just as enslaving. Our pettiness, our selfishness, our priorities make gods of the superficial. Spiritual surrender is the only way to destroy these gods.

It is not until we can say from the depth of our being, "I need help," that inner healing can begin. Jesus excoriated the Pharisees because they denied they were sick. He refused to minister to them because they said they were well and needed no physician.[2] The drunkards, the prostitutes, the social-

45

ly benighted, the despised tax collectors, and even the common people who lived lives of quiet desperation "heard him gladly."[3] They were open to the new life he gave because they were ready to surrender. The process of inner healing could begin with them because they knew their deep need.

Jesus never needed to speak in terms of surrender to those who knew they needed help. He called the thirsty to drink, the hungry to eat. One saint put it well when he said, "God would never come to a starving man as anything except bread to satisfy his hunger." God also might come to a "sleeping" man as shock to awaken him if, at the steering wheel of his life, he was dozing toward death. Life's crises intend to tell us, "Surrender to God or die."

PROGRESSIVE SURRENDER

We must not live under the illusion, however, that surrender is one single act. Many Christians feel that after they have discovered this new dimension of the Spirit, they have no need to yield their lives for the healing of the deep mind. The frequent disclaimer is "Inner healing is unnecessary for me; Christ healed me when he saved me." Others say, "I don't see any need for inner healing. I'm perfectly happy the way I am." There is a note of dangerous spiritual complacency in such attitudes.

Every un-Christlike attitude or action should be examined as a symptom of an unhealed aspect of our inner child. Since God is perfect love and never withholds any aspect of his love from anyone, the only conceivable reason we ever manifest spiritual poverty in our conduct is when something within us refuses

46

to receive, or is incapable of receiving the love God wants to lavish on all of us.

In the home, a wife may try to explain away her unhappiness. She may feel that her poorly veiled bitter words toward her husband are a product of overwork and lack of attention. This is not true. The time will have to come when she sees her bitterness as a sign of rebellion. Only then will she be able to face her own problem.

The husband who comes home from the office and chews out the children for not getting their homework done, or makes a snide comment about the meal his wife serves, and wonders why he generally is being robbed of the happiness he deserves because his wife and children don't seem to treat him right is in this same situation. He must come to the point of surrender. He must see as truly as Bob, the corporation executive, that even though he may have experienced the love of Christ, his everyday behavior is in rebellion against God. He must recognize that sooner or later he is going to have to kneel before the Christ of truth. He will have to yield to the truth, surrender to the truth that he is the real problem and recognize that only God can set him free.

Husbands and wives who continually blame each other or the children for their problems should consider the experience of Mary H. In Mary's frustration she had drifted from one religious group to another trying to deepen her spiritual life. She knew that Christ was supposed to be her satisfaction, but her dissatisfaction kept growing. When she heard about an inner healing retreat she thought it was simply one more religious retreat. Since she felt the need for another shot in the arm, she registered.

Some Christians hop from conference to conference hoping that one more weekend of inspiration will lift them over the top and forever out of their emotional "gray funks." Too often the conference experience is just a temporary palliative, an aspirin tablet, that fails to heal the root cause. But Mary discovered at the end of the inner healing workshop that the leader was pointing a spotlight on a shadowed area of her life that she had never been aware of before. Jesus said, "You shall know the truth and the truth shall make you free."[4] But the truth about one's self can make one extremely nervous before it makes one free.

Through a prayer for inner healing, Mary was led back to her childhood relationship with her mother. Mother was a constant complainer. But before Mary was able to experience any release from this childhood wound, she wrestled with herself through the first night of the conference. In her thoughts, she mocked the leader, condemning her as unspiritual. But the Spirit was at work within, and before she was able to sleep, she said to God, "If my frustration is caused by something unseen by me, then help me to see it. I'll be willing to be washed in the muddy water of the Jordan. And that's what all this inner healing seems like to me. Muddy water."

That kind of prayer is surrender. And that is what led to the insights that came bursting to the surface of Mary's mind as a simple prayer for inner healing was given by the leader. She suddenly saw why she bitterly complained over the most petty things which happened between her and her husband. Instead of seeing herself as a mistreated housewife, she saw that she was playing a "tape recording" made of material she had heard from her unhappy mother.

Mary wept in confession to God that she had blamed her husband and children for something that <u>had come out of her own heart.</u> She then saw herself embraced by a woman so beautiful that she could only have been a divine image of perfect womanhood. As this Marylike figure embraced her, she sensed what her womanhood was meant to be. No doubt she will have to encounter the old irritableness and complaining spirit many times, and each time surrender to that higher vision of womanhood. But this continual surrender is the creative staircase to maturity. And it must be taken one step at a time.

REBELLION IN YOUTH

Many young people become rebels, enemies of Christ, because they find emotional involvement and commitment threatening. This is sometimes caused by fathers who have been incapable of showing personal warmth and maturity to their children. The absence of a secure, affectionate father caused Tom to reach out for some significant male in his life to fill this void.

Tom found himself being drawn to a Christian leader, a man who seemed to him to be everything he would like to have had in a father. The attachment was not homosexual. It was the deep longing of Tom's inner child reaching out to a man he had idealized. He had been raised in a military home where his father, an officer in the Air Force, had seen a great deal of overseas duty during Tom's early childhood.

When the older man began to believe that the attachment was unhealthy, he decided to make no contact by telephone or letter. Tom's reaction was violent. And for five years he lashed out against himself, his friends, and the world. Friends were shocked when they heard he was involved in drugs and one wild feminine relationship after another.

Tom continued to run until, in emotional exhaustion and spiritual despair, he started looking for new answers. At that point he came in contact with a group of young former drug users and heard them talk about the joy they had found in Christ. One of the members, a former self-proclaimed guru in a West Coast commune, had experienced healing from a similar parental void. Dan was a warm and caring human being. He, too, had never known a father but, he told Tom, the qualities of manhood had been revealed to him in the manhood of Jesus Christ. A sense of Christ's personal presence had come through prayer, meditation, and the Scriptures. And quite suddenly he had realized one day what Jesus meant when he said, "He who has seen me has seen the Father."[5] That abstract phrase which had disturbed him before, "the Fatherhood of God," burst upon his consciousness as a vibrant reality.

Dan knew the wonder of Fatherhood, but he said to Tom, "Everyone learns the lessons of life in different ways. I'd like to pray that your emotions may be healed and that you may discover a new relationship with your dad. This is faith, Tom. God can make love exist where it just didn't, because he is Love."

During a group meeting, Dan led Tom back into his earliest childhood with care and precision. He helped him erase the old unhappy memories of rejection, first of an absent father, and then of a father present with him who didn't seem to care. Through visualization, reinforced by faith, Dan helped Tom experience a loving, responsible, strong father. He saw his daddy lifting little three-year-old Tom into his arms.

That was all Tom could handle. He began to tremble and weep. But it was enough. The group of young men gathered around him and began to express their appreciation of him. They asked him to lie down on the floor so they could lift him up and cradle him in their locked arms. As they rocked him, they sang the hymn, "Father we adore you/ Lay our lives before you/How we love you."

SURRENDERING VICES (THE DARK SIDE)

Fear of the unknown is a frequent experience of a little child. Footsteps walking down a corridor are those of a terrible monster and the child trembles in dread. Then when the door opens it is mother coming to say goodnight. Strange sounds outside the bedroom window at night come from a horrible ghost trying to get in. The child dives under the covers to hide. The morning light reveals the phantom was only the tree branches in the wind beating against the side of the house.

Similar fears haunt adult emotions. Deep within us there are stirrings which seem to threaten our security, our integrity, our sanity. When we realize that many of these fears are ugly emotions seeking to be loved into beauty, the fearful ghosts of the mind become as harmless as the windblown tree outside our childhood window.

A young lady asked a prayer group to pray for her problem, but she was too embarrassed to admit its identity. When the leader tactfully suggested that her problem might be her excess weight, she lamented, "Right. And I've done everything I can to lose weight and just can't. I've tried diet pills, fasting, prayer. Nothing seems to work. The harder I try, the fatter I get."

When it was suggested that she might be starving for affection, the young woman responded that she did want more love than she was getting. She was told not only to accept but also to give thanks for her obesity. This made sense to her when she could see that she was blessed with a strong desire for the sweetness of life and love. Being able to give thanks for what appears to be a mortal enemy by looking it straight in the eye makes surrendering possible. That which seems to be destroying happiness can become the catalyst for healing. When one gives thanks, an amazing metamorphosis usually takes place, like a butterfly emerging from an ugly gray cocoon. The condition that appears to be ugly, like the childhood ghost, has within it a hidden, rich beauty.

This overweight young lady's self-image was that of a gluttonous fat girl. She didn't realize that her behavior fed this image, perpetuating a vicious cycle. By living in the negative image, she fulfilled it, driving away the love of others. This negative response toward people, especially men, was reinforced as she cushioned herself behind a layer of fat from affectionate advances anyone would want to make toward her. In other words, she literally was hiding behind a wall of fat. By being physically less attractive, she was less able to accept love.

In reality, she was saying by her behavior, "I want desperately to fill that heart-shaped void. If food is the only substance available to fill it, then I have to eat." By surrendering to her obesity and by recognizing that she was not a glutton but simply starved for love, it gradually became possible for her to accept herself and to express and receive love.

Who but Jesus might have imagined that the real drive of the prostitute that anointed his feet was this same insatiable desire—to be loved by God?[6] We need to learn that always behind a negative goal is a positive one. Jesus told us, "Do not lay up for yourselves treasures on earth"—the negative goal —"but lay up for yourselves treasures in heaven"— the positive goal.[7] St. Paul said, "Do not get drunk with wine"—the negative goal—"but be filled with the Spirit"—the positive goal.[8] This is simply another way of saying, don't try to destroy that dark side of yourself, but surrender it to God. Don't judge and condemn it, but surrender it to God. Most of all, don't try to deny you have it. *Embrace the prodigal quality in you.* The avaricious man can become the enthusiastic seeker after spiritual riches; the drunkard can become a God-intoxicated lover of men. Every vice is a virtue which has lost its way.

Untold millions suffer inconsolably under the tyranny of guilt. The liar does not realize that he or she simply wants acceptance and affirmation. The gossips want the same thing they criticize others for because they are often bored with their own existence. They need to see the significance of their own lives. They don't need to degrade another in order to exalt themselves. The man with the violent, uncontrollable temper doesn't realize that he is lashing out at himself; he doesn't know that that temper is a perverted will to perfection. The anger which drove Saul of

Tarsus to torture and kill good men was the same energy which, when surrendered to Jesus Christ, drove him to sainthood.

DANGER OF DENYING VICES

Our society has been poisoned with the idea that moralizing can eliminate vices. To one who has never surrendered, moralizing frequently compounds the problem by causing one to refuse to admit the vice, and by increasing the twin burdens of guilt and rebellion.

Repressed negativity can be extremely dangerous. This is the combustible material out of which many emotional breakdowns and much antisocial conduct explode. On the other hand, to express negativity and make another person the victim of our vice, and then to have it condoned, increases the damage to the assailant and the victim.

The importance of surrendering our vices to God cannot be overstated.

Embracing and surrendering one's dark side is not to be confused with immorally blind permissiveness. Spiritual surrender demands that we look at the dark condition and see its imperfect and deadly potential. A scientist who wishes to create the life-giving substance salt in the laboratory must use sodium, which is a deadly mineral, and chlorine, a lethal gas. But when the two are brought together under controlled conditions, they become salt. Similarly, the imperfect and misdirected elements of our dark side when brought together with acceptance and surrender to God produce positive and bright characteristics.

DEALING WITH UNCONTROLLABLE SEX FEELINGS

One subject which, until recently, rarely saw the light of honest discussion is the subject of masturbation. In the past, young people were warned in unsubstantiated moralizing that masturbation would cause everything from pimples to insanity. In the minds of some, it seemed to be the unforgivable sin. No consideration was given to the fact that youths are thrown into a sex-oriented society where movies, magazines, and Madison Avenue all use sexually stimulating material in a generally irresponsible manner. Any young person with normal sex drives feels the frustration of being sexually alive and even aroused in today's culture. Few Christian voices have been raised offering a sympathetic and realizable answer to the question, "What do we do with all of these sex feelings?"

A few youths blessed with a large amount of parental love and personal creativity are able to live happily with healthy sexual control. But the majority of youths feel guilty about their erotic feelings.

Our youth must be taught that sexual feelings are God-given. They must learn that for a man to desire a woman sexually or a woman to desire a man is normal, and that until a high level of spirituality is attained, these feelings must be ventilated. It is only partially true that if more athletics or strenuous muscle exercises are made a part of one's discipline, sexual expression is unnecessary. Depending on a person's temperament, outlet through activity will have a varying degree of success. Other youths have been told that if they accept Jesus Christ, such feelings will be controlled. This is patently false. Many of these youth have run to marriage believing that, perhaps, marriage will alleviate the problem. It can be a devastating disappointment to find that these purported solutions usually solve nothing. They may resolve the problem for a few, but most remain plagued by guilt and frustration.

But there is a solution for those who have found no other resolution for uncontrolled sexual feelings. It is surrender. The first step is to embrace your dark side, your sexual self. It is significant that the ancients described the genital level of the human body as the sacral level. The words *sacral* and *sacred* come from an identical root word meaning "of divine origin," "devoted to God." Sexual energies, when first blossoming within the body, cause the transformation of a baby-fat boy into a sturdy man, a gawky, angular girl into a lovely, appealing woman. In his book *Think and Grow Rich*,[9] Napoleon Hill has taken this idea one step further. He says that he has never seen a truly successful man who was not a highly sexual man who had learned properly to direct his sexual energies. Ultimately this basic drive is the power of God. With this understanding we are able not only to live comfortably with our sexuality but to be grateful for it. We can give thanks that we will grow and mature to the place where it will be the power motivating us to highest creativity.

Susan grew up in a devout Catholic family. When she arrived at her teen years, she was horrified by her sexual feelings. On the few dates she permitted herself, she was able to abstain from intercourse. She enjoyed some controlled and frustrating petting but found herself, after returning home, yielding to sexual fantasies and then to masturbation. Her guilt drove her to greater acts of contrition and religious activity. Because she was sincerely devout, because she wanted to serve God and believed that God would never use one as unclean as she felt, she decided to join a religious order. Surely, she felt, behind the walls of a convent, there would be escape from the world of sensuality and temptation. But after becoming a novitiate, she found that instead of less sexual compulsion, she felt more. This led to greater feelings of guilt. Worse, she felt that she couldn't even expose this part of her life in confession.

At a point when Susan had almost abandoned hope of ever finding release, she attended a religious conference where one of the speakers dealt with the subject of inner healing. She was stunned to hear the speaker talk openly and with compassion about the matter of masturbation and other sexual problems. She heard her say that Jesus Christ was not primarily concerned with ridding one of the habit. His great concern was to reach into the heart of the plagued individual and heal what was broken and imperfect. The speaker reminded the audience that the subject of masturbation was of such little concern to Jesus that it is never recorded that he ever said a single word about it, though no doubt it existed. The bright side of this act, she added, is that it points to a thirst for love. So, instead of any condemning word, in compassion Jesus said, "If any one thirst, let him come to me and drink."[10] Nor did he say specifically what a person might thirst after; he just said, "If you thirst, come to me."

The speaker went on to explain that in the childhood experience of sexual experimentation often there is the trauma of parental condemnation and punishment. The helpless child learns the perverted lesson that sex and sexual feelings are evil rather than a God-ordained experience of self-discovery.

Susan sat there spellbound. Every word, she felt, had been spoken just to her. But the most shocking, yet hopeful, revelation of the day came when the speaker asked the audience, "How many of you have suffered unresolved guilt caused by the habit of masturbation?" Honest hands were lifted all through the auditorium. She thought she had been the only person ever to suffer such sexual guilt.

Until that day, Susan had never allowed the memories of her early sexual experimentation to linger in her thinking. She had repressed them. But when the prayer for inner healing was offered, Susan visualized a scene where Jesus and his mother Mary met Susan in her bedroom. There, as she was transported through imagination back into her early childhood, she was discovering her physical body. She looked up to see her Lord warmly smiling at her. She felt Mary lean over and press a kiss upon her forehead. At that point she surrendered herself to Jesus. In her imagination she felt Jesus lift her naked body into his arms and, for the first time, she felt clean.

People who find themselves obsessed by the habit of masturbation might accept the fact that Jesus Christ lovingly awaits the surrender of their own sexual image. It is as though he says, "Masturbate as long as you must. When you are ready to surrender I will lead you to a higher place. While you are in the valley of whatever shadow may be across your life, still I am with you, ready to lead you into the light as soon as you surrender to my guidance."

4.

The Healing Power of
FORGIVENESS

Forgiveness is at the heart of Jesus' message and it is at the heart of inner healing. But so much which needs to be forgiven is a part of our distant past. How can we forgive the forgotten? If our Christian life is contaminated by unforgiven pain inflicted upon us by incidents and people we don't remember—and it is—what can we do about it? When pain too agonizing to be borne has been inflicted upon a little child and the traumatic experience has been repressed, sealed in the vault of forgetfulness, how can the memory ever be brought out into the light and dealt with? How can anyone forgive something buried so deeply? Inner healing, through Christ's love, provides answers to these questions.

BEGINNING THE PROCESS OF FORGIVENESS

Before hidden bitterness can be exposed and transformed, remembered unforgiveness has to be dealt with honestly. Like an explosive antipersonnel mine, buried and unreleased antagonism is usually wired by our emotions to be triggered by something on the surface of our life. The act of forgiving a wrong of more recent creation on the conscious level will not automatically heal the past situation. But, following the imagery of the mine, if the immediate event can be defused, we then can trace the wiring back to its explosive, half-buried source. Then the root condition can be perceived and removed.

When an immediate situation seems impossible to forgive, it usually points to a root cause in one's childhood. The bitterly rejected child needs only to have a minor or even imaginary experience of rejection as an adult to bring on latent violent emotional reactions. The victim of constant overcontrol in childhood will feel immense anger and frustration when, as an adult, relatively benign overcontrol is experienced. But no matter how difficult it may be to forgive the immediate offender, it must be done. Deep inner healing will be frustrated until we have forgiven. And if our emotions cannot respond with the wisdom of forgiveness, our wills can. So if a review of our past life indicates that we have not forgiven someone, enlightened self-concern dictates that we had better prepare ourselves to be about the business of forgiving. If we refuse to forgive, we the offended will lose more than the offender.

BECOMING WHAT WE CAN'T FORGIVE

By rejecting another person and refusing to forgive, we are refusing to look at the root problem within ourselves. The consequence of such action is deeper repression of our personal weakness and an increased tendency to express that weakness without realizing it.

Whatever we cannot forgive we are doomed one day to live. The person who refuses to forgive the gossip eventually becomes a gossip. The one who cannot forgive a betrayal becomes a betrayer. The reason for this is that the inability to forgive a frailty in another person indicates that we have the same negative condition existing in us. If we had forgiven that weakness in another, the act of forgiveness would have acted as an antidote to our own weakness. But our willingness to forgive fertilizes the seed of that ugly quality within us.

It was the understanding of Carl Jung that the "dark side" of an individual, or that unseen, unaccepted facet of one's personality, contains immense power to control conduct from the unconscious level—until that darkness is embraced. Might this be the psychological principle that lies behind the tragedy of Judas Iscariot? If we look at his betrayal of Jesus in light of this principle, could we not assume that he had experienced bitter betrayal somewhere in his earlier life and had been unwilling to forgive his betrayer? Was he bound compulsively to play the role of the betrayer because he had not forgiven?

Some people believe that God made Judas a fall guy, that he was forced by some divine fiat to live out the role of Christ's betrayer. If Judas was the victim of his own unforgiving spirit, it could be that Jesus understood this dark quality and referred to it when he turned to Judas at the Last Supper and said, "What you are going to do, do quickly."[1] If Judas had surrendered his unforgiving spirit to Jesus, that could have provided the clearest channel for his own personal blessing. In the Lord's Prayer we are told to pray, "Forgive us our debts, as we also have forgiven our debtors."[2] The implication of this invocation is not that God awaits our act of forgiveness of another before he is willing to forgive us. That would contradict the truth that God is love. What Jesus is telling us is that as we forgive, our hearts are more open to receive the forgiveness of God which has always been available. Many people who have struggled with unrelenting guilts and fears need only to forgive those who have offended them to find immediate release from guilt and a fresh flow of peace and joy within.

THE POWER OF PENITENCE

The power of penitence is the other side of the coin of forgiveness. When we come to see our own authentic guilt within, as offender, and seek the forgiveness of the one we have offended, our own heart is brought into intimate healing touch with the heart of Christ. And the one from whom we have asked forgiveness is challenged to respond to penitent, vulnerable humility. If that person responds to us with forgiveness, a full and complete circle of creation out of chaos is experienced.

The story of Betty Lou graphically demonstrates this truth. She hid her emotional leprosy behind pious façades. She was nice on the outside, and uptight and hypercritical on the inside. A devoted church worker and community do-gooder, she was miserable. Frequently ill because of the constant emotional tension under which she lived, she had no idea why she was so unhappy and unreal. But she grew to feel such self-contempt that she started looking for answers.

When I met her at a seminar on inner healing, she was a scarred and frightened veteran of two nervous breakdowns, had a grown daughter who recently had almost been killed in an auto accident and another daughter who had just gone through a separation from her husband. She lived in constant fear of recurring bouts with insanity. The list of woes goes on like a poorly written soap opera. She was desperate!

In a letter received four months after the workshop experience she wrote:

"When you asked us to imagine the time before birth, I realized that I did not want to be born. I was frightened and didn't want to face this big empty world apart from my mother's womb. I developed a terrible headache during the prayer . . . it was like my skull was being crushed. Then I saw Jesus standing over me in my imagination, praying for me. The pain went away. And then I saw myself being born into a beautiful new world with Jesus there beside me and I knew that he would be there with me at all times. . . .

"In the prayer when we were visualizing our life at the age of three I remembered the terror of being taken to the doctor and the fear engendered by being told that a black doctor would punish me if I were bad. [Here was Betty Lou's first contact with prejudice and related fear.]

"At age five, with Jesus standing beside me, I recalled the anger of being ignored by my mother because she had time only for my older sister who had hepatitis and had been bedridden for over a year.

"Suddenly I remembered a terrible scene where my father in a rage threw an ice pick at my mother and hit her in the shoulder—where the ice pick stuck in and dangled from her flesh. At that moment, Jesus cradled me in his arms, and rocked me and told me that he loved me.

"At this moment of meditation we were told to imagine Jesus kneeling before us. I couldn't, because I had been taught that he was a punishing God, a God of wrath and severity—like doctors—and blacks —and that I wasn't worthy of Jesus' love.

"While as a little child I could imagine Jesus cradling me in his arms, I could not imagine him kneeling before me as an adult.

"At this point I couldn't take the emotional pressures, and I got up and ran from the room.

"I went directly to the prayer room where I was alone—but I still felt Christ's presence. A hundred forgotten images crowded in on my memory—of the terrible childhood fears instilled into me by stories I had heard on the farm. Suddenly all my fears of blacks added up to attitudes of prejudice and bigotry and genuine pharisaism. I had never admitted this to myself and I began to remember some experiences with blacks which kept me from being the loving person I so wanted to be.

"Oddly enough the terror of this new awareness and the self-revulsion that it caused brought me into a peace and calm I never had experienced before.

"As I walked from the meeting out into the lobby

I saw a tall, burly, broad-shouldered young man who looked like a football tackle. This man radiated a physical power that could almost be felt as I approached him. I stopped and stared at him. I was filled with fear. He was very black—the epitome of all that I had been taught to fear as a child.

"As I stood there, I heard a voice within me say: 'Go ask his forgiveness. Don't be afraid. I'm right beside you.'

"I hesitated: why should I ask this black, a total stranger against whom I had never done anything, for forgiveness?

"But I obeyed the inner voice. I went up to him. All I could say was, 'Forgive me,' and I burst into tears. Between sobs I told him of my fears, my upbringing, and that I was truly sorry.

"He reached out and took me into his arms, and comforted me, and said:

" 'It's all right, sister. I forgive you. It's okay. I love you.' "

Betty Lou's penitence called forth the forgiveness of a total stranger. She was healed, a new relationship was established, and a world created from chaos came one giant step closer to the kingdom of love through the miracle of forgiveness.

HEAD VERSUS HEART FORGIVENESS

I cannot overstate the value of the *will* to forgive—that is, the act of forgiving without the feeling of forgiveness. But it is necessary to guard against the notion that merely verbalizing an "I forgive" is enough.

Sometimes that is a way of saying, "I can't handle

you and what you did to me. But so that I can live with my neurotic conscience, I'm mouthing the words, *I forgive,* but I can't really forgive you."

Millie lived in such an illusion. She thought she had forgiven. But the gift of inner healing to her was the discovery that she had not forgiven and that she had the ability to do so. I wept when she described the loneliness and the fear of people which she had endured for sixty-seven years. She had committed her life to Christ at the age of ten and had lived "obediently by faith," doing charitable work, supporting benevolent causes, and seeking always to honor Christ through service. But Millie confessed she had never felt love—not for Christ, not for people.

She attended many retreats and religious conferences hoping that one day she might experience release from her torment. She always returned home disappointed, empty and plagued with an ever-present loneliness. But she heroically kept serving Christ. Her life of commitment was based on pure faith. She felt absolutely nothing.

As tenderly as I could, I began to question her.

"Do you make friends easily?"

"No."

"Do you ever feel close to people?"

"No."

"Do you like people to show you affection?"

"They never do."

"Do you ever hug people affectionately?"

"I can't remember ever hugging anyone."

I pursued this, but she could not remember one time since her early childhood when she had touched another person, for even so much as a handshake. There is the likelihood that she had had experiences of touch but some acute emotional pain blocked out the memories.

Her father, whom she had dearly loved, had been committed to an asylum when she was only six years old. He was never released, and died there about twenty-five years later. Before their tragic separation, her father, a poet and musician, would hold her for hours in his lap, quoting little rhymes he had composed just for her. Her face brightened as she recalled how he would often sing songs and play his violin for her, sometimes creating a tune right there. But the light left her face as she told us that often in the midst of a song he would change quite suddenly and grow violent.

Sobbing, she buried her face in her hands as she relived an experience she had had at age six. She began to tremble as she recalled how he grabbed her by the throat and held a knife to it. Just as the knife was penetrating her skin, her grandfather wrestled him to the floor and took the knife away. That was the day they took her father away.

As Millie shared her story, a young doctor sitting with us found her pain more than he could bear. He walked over to where she was sitting, and took her in his arms. The moment he embraced her, something happened in her. With eyes closed, she sobbed, "O Daddy, I love you! I love you. I forgive you for hurting me. I forgive you!"

Realizing what was happening, the doctor continued in the assumed father role and expressed what might have been her father's words of love: "Millie, my darling, I never meant to hurt you. I was so sick. Thank you for forgiving me. I love you, my precious child."

For the next fifteen minutes the "father" and daughter experienced their love in silence and gently shared endearments. When Millie opened her eyes and withdrew from the doctor's arms, I knew Jesus had walked into the depths of her heart. She said that she had been sure that she had forgiven her father. But the drama we had just witnessed made it clear that until this day the forgiveness had never come from the inner child of the past.

During the rest of the conference Millie's fear of people was diminished. She was able to give love as well. She began to make friends for the first time since her childhood. Once the forgiveness of her father had moved from her head to her heart, she could feel loved, and life was once again worth living.

A Test of Forgiveness

The need to forgive authentically, totally, always raises the question, "How can I know whether I have really forgiven someone or whether I am deceiving myself?" As a general rule the question should not even concern us. We should assume that when we forgive we are really forgiving. It is only when warning signs appear that we ought to consider the possibility of a problem. If bitter thoughts about the one we forgave keep surfacing or if, as in the case of Millie, we have an emotional handicap we can't overcome—such as fear of men, lingering resentments, inability to cope with certain types of people, to name only a few—it could indicate the need to reassess the reality of our forgiveness. At all times we must believe that God is guiding our insights when we are seeking the truth. "The Spirit," said Jesus, "will guide you into all the truth."[3] And that includes the truth about forgiveness in our life.

If we have any uneasiness about a person we once had to forgive, there is a simple, clear way of checking out the situation. Visualize yourself in the situation where you were offended. Then see the person who hurt you standing before you. Now bring Jesus into the scene and ask him to go behind the once guilty party. Then try to see the two figures merge into one. If Jesus readily flows into your former offender, it is a sure sign that no further forgiveness is needed. If Jesus does not flow into the person, continue to imagine the two images and work with them each day. Eventually true forgiveness will be realized.

A prayer asking God to forgive your antagonism may be all that is needed. Try it. Then check again to see if Jesus can enter the person. If he still cannot, it usually indicates the need for more radical action. A safe but momentarily shocking way to proceed is to visualize yourself receiving a sword from the hand of Jesus and running it through the heart of the unforgiven. This vividly and honestly expresses any unrecognized, residual hatred that may remain in your heart that has frustrated forgiveness. Then let Jesus breathe into the person, kneeling in healing love over the fallen form. This expresses your forgiveness and love. Now, amazingly, Jesus will enter the form of the one you had not really forgiven.

It is important and healthy to realize that this is not a desire to kill that other person but to kill the anger within yourself. The results are always positive because the negative bondage of anger in a relationship is destroyed. This technique, more radical than the first test, should be periodically used until forgiveness takes place and there is no emotion of anger toward the other person. The miracle of honest emotion expressed, followed by sincere forgiveness offered, produces the healing of the wound in the heart which had resisted repair.

THE FEAR OF FORGIVING

A frequent blockage to the healing flow of forgiveness is not hate but fear. When emotional pain is inflicted, especially by someone close to us, the anxiety frequently arises, "If I forgive them, I am granting them the license to hurt me again." We may know Jesus' instruction that we must be willing to forgive "seventy times seven" times a day.[4] The instinct of self-preservation, that primitive, practical ego trip, takes charge. Something within feels so threatened that our only thought is to get out of the emotional range of the person who has inflicted the hurt and get into a shell of safety. Two things can save this kind of situation: if we are the offender we can love and reach out our hand to the frightened until trust is regained; or as the offended we can ask that God will not allow us to be destroyed. We know that it is essential to be obedient to Christ's command to forgive no matter how often we are hurt. We must live in reliance on God's protection.

A young couple who came to me for counseling loved each other as fervently as any two I had ever seen. But they were confronted with what they felt was the ultimate crisis of their married life. He accused her of fabricating problems. She was overly jealous, he said, and would constantly assault him for emotional crimes against her which he never committed. She replied that he was unbearably sensitive and overreacted at her slightest criticism. After listening to their problem, I asked him, "You said you couldn't stand any more of her hostility. If she continues to be hostile what do you intend to do?"

"I don't know. That's my frustration," he responded. "I love her so much and I know she loves me, but man do we fight!"

"We've prayed," the wife said, "and tried until we're very tired and discouraged."

When I inquired into their spiritual experience, I found that it was not run of the mill. They both expressed their devotion to God. Both had an unusually deep faith in Jesus Christ.

"Then I can tell you," I concluded, "and I know you will understand. Jesus is your only hope. The depth and complexity of your problem isn't going to be solved overnight. But if each of you can do for the other what Christ has done for you—forgive you no matter how often or gravely you offend him—you'll make it. God has answers for you. But his first answer is 'Forgive.'"

Theirs was not a "They lived happily ever after" story. I see this couple almost once a month. They still love each other. They still fight. And they still are growing. They share insights they are gaining. And as a ringside spectator, I am convinced that both of these heavyweight fighters are going to win.

FORGIVING OUR PARENTS

The discovery of emotional root problems can sometimes lead to an unhealthy reaction—we tend to blame our parents too harshly. And usually they are involved in our early traumas, because Mother and

Daddy constitute our whole emotional world during those early formative years.

We need to understand as adults that there is purpose and design in our universe. The Father of our Lord Jesus Christ knew the kind of parents we needed in order to become his completed child. When the Psalmist says that God knew him and formed him in his mother's womb, he was affirming that the Lord was his shepherd in his mother's womb, too.[5] God did not make a mistake.

To accept this truth is to learn an amazing consequent fact. Not only did we need our parents' love and care to become the uniquely beautiful persons God wills us to be, but we also needed their weaknesses and even sinful traits. Our reactions to their weaknesses and sins are a positive part of God's creative process. Isaiah says that God's ways are not our ways.[6] Obviously his vision of our completed personalities, our ultimate perfection, is not our vision. Are we willing to surrender our vision of our own personality to his? Forgiveness is the doorway.

We must first forgive by faith. We must believe that God is love and would not inflict meaningless chaos. The result of such an act of faith will be the revelation of the creative power of suffering.

But such an exalted understanding always comes after the fact of forgiveness. And when it comes, it comes with a certainty which makes the saddest childhood flood with light. Gratitude that we could be given exactly the right parents for us follows forgiveness.

Remember when you judge your parents' deficiencies that your negative reactions are a part of your personality that God wants you to release. His vision of you requires these negatives to be chiseled away.

And if the chiseling of this Sculptor of our soul has seemed painful or unnecessary, we need only look at the pile of chipped marble at the feet of Michelangelo's "David" as it is being completed in his Florentine studio to know that the mastermind will also bring forth his masterpiece from the block of unshaped marble that is our self.

THE DEATH OF A PARENT

The death of a parent is a childhood crisis which often has subtle but devastating results in later life. It is a problem because usually by adolescence the child has rationalized the parent's death and has concluded, "That is just one of those things. My parent died and I'll just have to make the best of it." But a far different monologue is taking place on the heart level. There the child is crying, "Why did Mommy (or Daddy) leave me? Why did they go and never come back? I needed them so. And they failed me!"

The inner child has no philosophy of life after death. It can't understand that the parent was a victim of circumstances. All it knows is feeling, a feeling of abandonment, a feeling of rejection. That shaking of the child's secure world can create a tidal wave in adult relationships. Until the inner child can face the anger created by the parental death and forgive that parent, the feeling of rejection causes the adult to anticipate rejection from others. Such an attitude is especially difficult in the marriage relationship. The anger of the inner child causes it to want to hold at a distance the one it wants to love. But even in less significant situations this attitude can cause tension and eroded relationships.

Another place where forgiveness is essential and

73

elusive is when parents have separated in one's childhood. This almost always registers as rejection in the child. A careful review of the feelings about each parent should be undertaken by any who went through the divorce of their parents. Listening to the angry arguments between mother and father can leave scars which must be removed by the Spirit. Children are frequently left with the guilt-ridden feeling that they caused the separation. In that case, the victim must not only forgive but must accept the forgiveness of God. It makes no difference that the guilt is not real. If it is felt, it must be treated as real. When the absolution is accepted and the guilt relieved, that usually is the time when an authentic reevaluation of feeling can take place.

FORGIVING GOD

Even God sometimes needs to be forgiven. An all-loving God would rather have our misdirected forgiveness because of misguided notions in order to establish a loving, trusting relationship with him and others as well as ourselves, than to be blocked by being shunned or scorned as an unloving God. Those who don't forgive God, feel guilty, very guilty. That causes the whole state of mind to deteriorate. When insight shows us that God is guiltless, we who have forgiven God can have a good laugh. But until we arrive at that understanding, forgiving God is no laughing matter. Only when we have done so will we be able to forgive ourselves for unjustly hating God.

So-called reasons for hating God are many. After all, he is the Ultimate Leader. Doesn't the buck stop with him? Isn't he the writer and producer of the show? If it is a flop, blame him! If we have poor health, if we are unattractive or unsuccessful, the easiest person to blame is God. If this kind of anger is there, then we should forgive God! As silly or irrational as it might seem to a theologian or an angel, how else can we establish a loving, trusting relationship with God than by acknowledging, in honesty, where we are? After we have forgiven him, then the likelihood of our loving him increases. All he needs is a chance to get his love through to us. Then we can begin to be more realistic.

FORGIVING OURSELVES

Forgiving God usually leads to the experience of forgiving the hardest of all persons to forgive—ourselves. And when we do that, we automatically start to love ourselves. Once we love ourselves, we begin to love everybody else. We react less severely to faults in others because we accept the imperfections in ourselves. And that is what the redeeming love of Christ and his divine forgiveness is all about.

5.

The Healing Power of CONFESSION

Guilt can lift us to nobility or torment us into hell. It all depends on what we do with it.

Without any pangs of guilt we could be amoral, destructive animals indulging in every conceivable inhumanity with no will to correct or let light into our dark ways. On the other hand, sensitivity to personal wrongdoing when ignored or perverted can build up immense poison which can cause many of the emotional and physical illnesses of the human race. When, for instance, guilt is heaped upon a child by an accusing parent or a punctilious church, it can distort this God-given sensitivity and create a beaten spirit who lives in fear of being threatened constantly. Or it can cause one to become an overbearing Pharisee bent on crushing others with relentless condemnation.

Persons seeking maturity try to pursue a balanced

midcourse between an immoral denial of personal guilt on the one hand and a deadly wallowing in it on the other. The latter binds us with the feeling that we are worthless sinful trash, that we are doomed to live with the fire of guilt burning out of control in our spirits.

JESUS' TREATMENT OF GUILT

Jesus' treatment of guilt was amazingly free of a spirit of condemnation. His deepest concern seemed to be for people who denied its existence within them—the Pharisees. This is in line with the best understanding we have today of the danger of repression. That is, a problem pushed down into our deep mind and covered from our conscious self becomes like a prowling killer whale, lurking under the surface of consciousness, hungry for something to attack and destroy. But lured into the shallows, studied and examined, that same whale can be tamed, used, fed and "domesticated." It loses its violence and even helps us develop and find fulfillment.

Jesus told the story about two men who came to church to pray. One, a very falsely pious type, "prayed with himself, 'God, I thank thee that I am not like other men'." (He thought he was better.) The second, broken man prayed in contrition, "God, be merciful to me a sinner." Jesus' telling comment was that the second man, not the first, went "to his house justified"—a righteous man.[1] Confession opened the door for the second man to receive the love and mercy of God.

CONFESSION AS A DIAGNOSIS

Honest confession is not an exercise in breast-beating; it is an act of honest exposure before God and man. It seems to have the same function that sound diagnosis has in medicine. It allows healing to be administered. But in the case of spiritual confession, the medicine is always therapeutic, and the Physician is never wrong or limited in his healing power. The idea of confession as diagnosis lies behind Jesus' words to the Pharisees when they denied that they were spiritually blind. A paraphrase of Jesus' response is, "Then there is nothing I can do for you; a physician only comes to the sick, that is, those who know they are sick."[2]

There is something refreshing and disarming about one who has nothing to hide. One can see this demonstrated in any Alcoholics Anonymous group. One of the rules of conduct for members of A.A. is "absolute honesty." The founders of this organization knew that there is no hope of remaining sober if the alcoholic insists on living a lie. They knew that human dignity cannot exist without honesty. Human dignity is found in our real worth as children of God, not in a false front erected to impress others.

ILLNESS FROM BURIED GUILT

The price of burying guilt can be unbearably high. It will take its toll on body and mind until the pressure is removed. The office of absolution—that is, the role of listening to the confession of another so that they may experience forgiveness—was the first group activity ordained by Jesus for the church after his resurrection. On the day of his resurrection he appeared to his disciples in the upper room where they were hiding. Standing among them he calmed their fears, and then, it is recorded, "he breathed on them, and said to them, 'Receive the Holy Spirit.'"

And immediately he gave as his first rule, "If you forgive the sins of any, they are forgiven."[3] Response to confession—release from guilt—was to be the first order of business.

When the church or society becomes unreal or uncaring, confession and release from guilt is the last order of business, the last thing it wants to get involved in. At a terrible cost, hiding behind masks becomes accepted, expected conduct. Covering up, hiding, playing a role insidiously cause all sense of relationship and community to disintegrate.

Our priority should be to rediscover confession and absolution. We are not free until we maturely share our guilt and responsibly release others from theirs.

In Capernaum, a city by the Sea of Galilee, Jesus was talking to a circle of religious leaders who had no understanding that religion without confession and compassion breeds death. There were such crowds following Jesus that for blocks around the house the streets were clogged with spectators trying to catch a glimpse of him. Within the mass of people, four men were on a mission of mercy. They had a friend who was paralyzed, and they were convinced Jesus could heal him. When they could not get near the front door, they climbed the stairway on the outside of the house, and on the roof they proceeded to lift up the tiles over the spot where Jesus was seated. The startled religionists watched as the hole grew larger and the four men carefully lowered their paralytic friend right in front of Jesus.

Seeing their faith he said, "My friend, your sins are forgiven you." The religious leaders were appalled. "Who is this man talking blasphemy? Who can forgive sins but God alone?"

Jesus knew that he had the authority to forgive

sin, but, more important, that his act released the
man from his guilt-related paralysis. So, he proved
his power dramatically. "Which of these is easier,"
Jesus asked them: "to say, 'Your sins are forgiven
you' or to say, 'Get up and walk'?" Of course, they
thought that to cause this local lame man to walk
would be the more difficult. They were wrong. The
single act of pronouncing forgiveness did both. And
Jesus confirmed this when he said, "But to prove
to you that the Son of man has authority on earth to
forgive sins,"—he said to the paralyzed man—"I order
you: get up, and pick up your stretcher and go
home." And immediately the forgiven man stood up
and made his way through a stunned, excited crowd
which parted to let him through.[4]

What Jesus did is now *our* task. Christ ordained
us to release the guilt-ridden. Recently I was in Latin
America working with a team of Catholics who were
ministering in a number of cities introducing people
to the living Christ and the power of the Spirit. A
man came to me for prayer whose throat was
partially paralyzed. For over twelve years he had
been unable to speak above a whisper.

As I put my hand on his throat and began to pray,
I perceived his problem. To confirm the insight the
Spirit had given, I asked him if he had been guilty
of a deep act of disobedience to God twelve years
ago.

A bit stunned, he answered immediately, "Yes."
When I asked him if it was something he would like
to confess, he replied, "No, it is not something I would
like to confess to you through a translator; please
find me a priest who speaks Spanish."

That night, after the man had made his confession,
he rose to speak to the group. His voice was loud

and clear as he stood before the people, sharing his reconciliation with Jesus, how after twelve years of self-imposed, guilt-created separation, he had found peace again. Then he told us how his confession had healed him in body and soul.

This man's throat condition is an example of the power of repressed guilt to damage the body and mind. The afflicted person who has pushed down guilt feelings cannot equate the paralysis, the headaches, the kidney infection or a whole catalog of diseases with a need to confess an old sin. The afflicted believes that he is just ill. But often there is a psychosomatic correlation. Could this be the reason for the early development of the synonym for *sickness, disease,* meaning dis-ease, a destruction or lack of inner peace? The refinement of psychosomatic medicine is revealing the accuracy of this assumption. The destruction of emotional ease and harmony by harbored guilt is the number one destroyer of health, of body and mind.

CONFESSION FROM A WHEELCHAIR

At a retreat a woman was brought to me in her wheelchair, paralyzed from the waist down and totally deaf. In order to make her more comfortable, her friends removed her from her chair and seated her on the sofa beside me. As I greeted her she read my lips. She then told me her story. She was a dedicated Christian, and though she did not believe her illness was physical, she could not pinpoint any emotional or spiritual cause. But if I would pray for her, she believed that the Holy Spirit would give me insight into its cause. As I listened I inwardly applauded her faith and honesty. These qualities always open healing doors.

I told her to close her eyes so that she could not lipread and so that her conscious mind would not know what I was saying, and I would pray with her spirit for the Spirit of Christ within her to reveal the cause. "Lord Jesus," I prayed, "let your Christ Spirit within her reach down into the hidden parts of her mind, into the deepest levels of her consciousness and reveal if there is any broken relationship, unforgiveness, guilt, sin or whatever else might cause her to be physically afflicted. Amen."

For nearly ten minutes she sat in silence. Then opening her eyes she said, "Ruth, God has told me. When I was a young girl I was a member of a large criminal operation with three other girls and I shoplifted a great deal of merchandise. Relative to my financial standing today, what was stolen is insignificant. But at the time, it was a great sin against God. I asked forgiveness many years ago, and then pushed it out of my mind. I just realized a few minutes ago that the reason I had dismissed these crimes as insignificant was so that I would not have to go to the owners and possibly have my husband discover what I had done.

"Tomorrow when this meeting is over, I must drive to another city and confess what I did to the various store owners face-to-face."

Then resolutely she pushed herself forward on the sofa, stood up, and took a few uncertain steps. Her walk was clumsy and somewhat uncoordinated, but she walked without help. Obviously she was not totally healed, but her healing had begun with the recall of her guilt, her confession, and the will to ask the forgiveness of her former victims.

PROGRESSIVE HEALING

Even in cases of psychosomatic illness, healing often comes in stages. As the heart absorbs the experience of forgiveness and release, the pathological condition frequently begins to disappear. Through further sharing, confession, and affirmation the Spirit peels away layer after layer of emotional infection. The final healing may occur weeks, even months after the first confession and counsel. But faithful application of James's instruction, "Confess your sins to one another, and pray for one another, that you may be healed,"[5] will always produce growth, healing and wholeness.

Any memories which have guilt overtones may need to be confessed. It is wise to omit nothing, however seemingly insignificant or petty. As we open our heart to the deep penetrating and probing of the Spirit's light, unremembered, unexpected memories of guilt can surface. Christian psychiatrist Paul Tournier says it is like entering a dimly lighted room. At first you see only the most evident and prominent things. But as you wait and your eyes become more accustomed to the dark, you realize that the room is filled with a clutter of objects. If the exposure is painful, it is healthy to rejoice in spite of the pain because of the new awareness. The more one relaxes in the certainty that God is at work, the more readily new insights will manifest themselves. Relaxation in the Spirit is a form of praise, and the power in this form is especially released when confronted in this context with personal guilt.

POSITIVE CONFESSION AND AFFIRMATION

When inner healing occurs through the act of confession, the healing should be affirmed repeatedly in the days following. This essential reinforcing process requires self-discipline. Whenever anything reminds one of the guilt confessed, the thought should be replaced gently with a scriptural affirmation such as, "If we confess our sins, he is faithful and just, and will forgive our sins."[6] This affirmation reminds the inner child that it is free, that it doen't need to return to chains that have been broken.

What we affirm today, we will become tomorrow—some tomorrow. If we claim that we are weak and infirm, we will become weak. If we repeatedly think in affirmative terms, we will rise to that level. A humble but powerful tool for maintaining mental and physical health is the affirmation. If we daily declare, "I am one with God and his Son Jesus Christ; his wholeness, power of mind and perfect peace are mine," we will contribute to our future health and happiness.

PERFECT LOVE CASTS OUT FEAR

Before I studied the subject of guilt, and observed persons who came seeking release from fear, I used to wonder why the New Testament says, "Perfect love casts out fear."[7] I thought that it would have been more logical to say that perfect love casts out its opposite—hate. Then I discovered that this is exactly what happens. When we feel grievously offended and we cannot forgive, our negative emotional quality deteriorates into hate. When we hate, the deep part of us knows that this dark emotion is wrong. Even when we consciously excuse ourselves, we grow to hate that part of ourselves when we hate another. We sense that we are offending that spirit of love—God—and we know, therefore, that we deserve to be punished.

If we have been led to believe that God is ready to crack down hard on sinners, it is especially terrorizing to defy the good. Our only relief is to punish ourselves. We live in the fear of punishment, so we do the job on ourselves. This can take the form of accident proneness. It can be an emotional punishment, such as paranoia, or compulsive cleanliness—like Lady Macbeth whose bloody hands she could not get clean as she washed them in her sleep and cried, "Out, damned spot!"

The momentary relief that does, in fact, come when we successfully punish ourselves is like the second shoe hitting the floor. "At last the whip has struck," we feel. "It can't surprise me now." But that sick relief is brief. The fear begins to grow and the process is repeated and continued until the root cause of the guilt is confronted and dealt with.

A woman who is a compulsive gambler has told me how she would continue to gamble until she had lost everything. Then she would feel a period of near ecstasy. She had punished herself. But the fear and self-loathing soon returned, and the wretched, vicious cycle would begin all over again.

This punishment process can explain many seemingly irrational acts, such as the homosexual who propositions a police officer when it is certain he will be arrested, or even why a wife will do everything in her power to enrage a jealous husband when she has been unfaithful. When he lashes out, when he beats her, she is relieved, she has been punished.

"The thing which I greatly feared is come upon me," said Job.[8] It usually does. But when punishment is feared, the later experience of pain is easier to endure than the suspenseful fear. Then how does love cast out fear? It simply eliminates the hate which creates the guilt which causes us to fear punishment for that guilt. So, of course, perfect love casts out fear by washing out the guilt-creating punishment necessitating hate. When we have nothing in our mind which seems to deserve punishment, then there is no fear of punishment. Confession clears the mind.

Unaccepted Forgiveness

Many victims of unrelieved guilt have not repressed their feelings. They have faced their guilt squarely, but they simply cannot stop facing it or feeling guilty about it even after confession. In that case, one usually must look beyond the specific deed which resists the release of confession to childhood conditioning. Not being able to accept forgiveness after confession usually means that mother failed in her primary role as a giver of unconditional, tender love. Mother's failure to lay a foundation of secure personal acceptance makes the stain of guilt take on the indelible quality Lady Macbeth knew. A child can learn much about the heart of God from the heart of his mother. If she is unforgiving of herself and consequently of the child, the adult barrier between inner child and a sense of forgiveness can be insurmountable without inner healing.

Anyone in this condition should pray for his or her mother and ask the Holy Spirit to reconstruct that early image of mother. One should pray that the spirit of perfect motherhood embodied in Jesus' mother Mary may capture the imagination and remake the unconscious understanding of unconditional love. When the new image is obtained, forgiveness is realized.

THE HEALING EFFECTS OF HEARING A CONFESSION

There is always personal blessing when one hears the confession of another out of commitment to Christ. But I discovered while listening to the confession of a convicted rapist that I, the listener, could be the learner and the greatest beneficiary of the confessional.

With humiliation and self-contempt he poured out his story. I sought to assure him that I understood —though I didn't. I told him Jesus was his healer and loved him unconditionally. That much I knew to be true. As I listened to the ugly story of perversion, hatred, and finally the ultimate abuse of a woman, I was sickened. I found it impossible to forgive when I couldn't comprehend what would motivate someone to descend to this bestial level. I found myself having to confess to God that I abhorred this young man confessing to me. As I listened to him, I had to confess my own rage. With my confession came compassion.

That young man helped me to expose my personal judgmentalism that I would have denied before this experience. "Oh yes," I had thought, "I love everyone, with no condemnation." But here in the role of loving, affirming, nonjudgmental confessor, I was compelled by God's love to deal with intense angers that had been repressed in my past. Now—suddenly— they were dealt with in a sacramental situation.

If we aspire to help others through the office of

confessor, we must ourselves be healed of subconscious needs to judge and condemn. When we undertake the office to discharge guilt, we are obliged to bring God's unconditional love to the guilt-bearer. At no point in spiritual relationships is James Russell Lowell's statement that "the gift without the giver is bare" more true than when the gift proffered is God's forgiving love.

CONFESSION AT HOME

Confessors, like prophets, tend to be without honor in their homes. And there is much religious tradition which dictates that confession is a priestly duty and should not be undertaken with members of one's own family. It is much easier to confess to the more distantly removed. But there are times when confession and openness are more important in our families than anywhere else. It takes some humility to share our flaws with mate and children. It also entails the risk of rejection in a significant relationship. But that is a risk we must dare to take.

For some time I had been fervently praying for my daughter. I could see that she was hurting badly and I told the Lord that *I* would rather hurt than have her suffer as she was. "Do anything necessary, Lord. But bring her the peace she needs."

It was not too long after this prayer that she said to me, "Mother, I'm really hurting. I'm in such pain I can't stand it, and I've got to talk to somebody."

I suggested several of my trusted, spiritually mature friends.

"No," she replied, "I can't talk to any of those people. It's got to be somebody that's been worse than I've been."

It was then I realized how much the other three of my children were like their father, and how much she was like me. And she was the one with whom I had most difficulty getting along. We frequently disagreed and had real difficulty communicating, while I found it easy to communicate and get along with my other children. But I also knew her better. I seemed to know what she was about to do before she did it. The reason was simple enough: she almost always responded to situations just as I did. With that special mother's inner eye, I could always see her wheels beginning to spin.

Three weeks before she came to me seeking help, I had prayed, "Lord, I want to be whole. And I want every member of my family to be brought into wholeness." In that prayer I especially had been imagining myself lifting this child into the stream of God's Spirit. *"Whatever it takes,"* I thought, "I release her into your hands even if I have to stand by and watch her suffer." Then in my thoughts appeared the idea, "You don't have to stand by, I'm going to let you get right in there and suffer with her because you are the only person that has lived such a similar life pattern."

Looking at her, I said, "Honey, you are going to have to confess to me. You see, your mother is not the perfect person I have tried to make you believe. In fact, that 'worse' person you've been looking for is"—I found it hard to say—"is me."

She stared at me in disbelief at hearing her spiritual leader mother say she was a first-rate sinner. She was sure it was maternal nonsense.

"Mother," she tested, "what's the worst thing you've ever done?" I didn't know what to say.

"Honey," I stammered, "let's go into the living room,

it's more private there . . . and before we start, let's turn all the lights off." In the darkness I held her hand.

Again she pressed, "Mother, tell me the worst thing that you ever did."

"I'm going to start with the first, not the worst, thing I ever did . . . and work up gradually."

Starting with events at ages four and five (that was the earliest I could remember), I went through every year of my life. I recounted all that came to me, from stealing a pencil in the first grade to the lies I had told to avoid punishment and the deceptions, the betrayals, the deeds toward those I had hurt. I even reviewed for her my many acts and attitudes of unforgiveness toward those who had hurt me. But as I began to open up for my daughter, memories of sins long forgotten and unconfessed poured to the surface.

When I got to age sixteen, I stopped. "I feel that's as far as it's fair for me to go, because you're only sixteen."

"Mother," she said, "that's as much as I can take. You really have been worse than me!"

"Okay, now," I said, "it's your turn."

So she began, sharing detail after detail. Strangely, from my somewhat more aged viewpoint I found it hard to agree that I had been worse. I saw our experiences simply as similar, almost identical. But from the position of a daughter hearing for the first time the failings of her mother, I can see how surely mine must have seemed worse.

In truth, our stories are similar to almost every person who has ever lived. We have all lied, but about different things. Everyone has stolen—perhaps not pencils, but cookies, or money. But how alike are the guilts of all members of the human race! "All have sinned," says the Bible "and come short of the glory of God."[9] How alike we are in the fact of sinning! And how far short of the glory of God have we all fallen! As I listened to myself telling, for the first time, each of my experiences, they didn't seem bad at all—merely life. They certainly didn't seem to justify the amount of guilt that had clung, leechlike, to the inner child of my being.

It was pure joy to see my daughter listen, love me, and respond to the long, painful review of my sins. Our relationship hasn't been the same since. An intimacy, a bond of trust was formed that day which has endured and grown with time. I would not exchange that experience for anything. How poorly we serve our children as they grow into adolescence and adulthood when we refuse to be vulnerable and honest about our weaknesses. There are few things more enriching than the love shared in parental confession.

There was another dividend. I was cleansed. I knelt to wash my daughter's feet and she helped to wash my soiled heart. Isn't God wonderful!

One of the colossal implications of his paradox—the last shall be first—was dramatized. The dishonorable role in the eyes of the world, performed in holy obedience, can be the most meritorious. Confession of dishonor in response to the Holy Spirit is transformed by him to a great and honorable exercise.

6.

The Healing Power of
SELF-ACCEPTANCE

One of the primary goals of inner healing is to help us accept ourselves, to inspire love for the self Jesus loves. I ignored this truth for many years and the consequences were depressing. My need for self-acceptance revealed itself only a few years ago. I found myself calling a friend about once a month to confess how much I had disappointed God and how unworthy of his love and forgiveness I felt. She would reassure me that God did love me, that he was not upset over what I had done, and that he was always ready to forgive. Each time I hung up the phone I felt a sense of relief. But then in a month or two I would call her back and say, "You won't believe what I have done this time."

Finally, after I had called several times and played back my record of self-contempt, she said, "Ruth, I think you have grown to the place now that what you really need to do is to get down on your knees and ask God to please forgive you for being a human being!"

Nothing could have been more impressively unexpected. Her statement jarred me onto a new road toward self-acceptance. On that road I found how much I had been conditioned to react to the pleasure or displeasure of others. I was myopic about what God wanted me to become because I was worried about how other people thought I should act. This attitude is common, I knew, but as a servant of Jesus Christ, I should be responding to life on a higher level than most. But to a dismally great degree I was not. I was denying my own growth potential.

PHYSICAL AND SPIRITUAL GROWTH

When we are born of the Spirit we become spiritual babies. We require care and nurture from other Christians who have had more experience in this life of faith and love. The danger is that we may become overcontrolled by these early spiritual parents. Out of misdirected concern they may not allow the new Christian to grow. Consequently, many spiritual infants are stamped into a cooky-cutter version of spiritual parents. Their unique development is lost and the whole church as well as the world is the loser.

Everyone loves babies. We cuddle them and hover over them with delight. Every sign of growth and change is a proud discovery. When the little one begins to walk and toddle, the event is greeted with pride and joy, even though by adult standards it is done poorly. Through each stage of the child's development, the loving parent is pleased to see one more evidence of growth toward independence.

So it is with our heavenly Parent, God. In our spiritual infancy, he accepts us as we are. As we develop, our progress may be imperfect, but he encourages faltering steps when we seek to walk with him. The years should bring increased competence. But God never condemns even a retarded child of his. We are to grow one step at a time, "looking to Jesus,"[1] not to anxious spiritual nannies. Unfortunately, we are too often influenced by our overcontrolling, religious babysitters.

Toe-the-mark-or-miss-the-mark attitudes stifle the creative power of the Holy Spirit. It is true that at the outset of the young Christian's spiritual pilgrimage proper and valuable nurture must be given. But many religious leaders find it difficult to relinquish their followers into the guiding hand of the Holy Spirit. "Feed my sheep," Jesus told Simon Peter.[2] He didn't say, "Mold and manipulate my untrustworthy people." Heavyhanded religious organizations and leaders inhibit free spiritual growth toward unique identity. The church is not the only institution holding this corrupting pattern. The home demands conformity to one set of values, the school to another, the peer group to another, and sometimes the government to still another. After we end our balancing act, trying to ride the crest of all demands for conformity, there is little chance for us clearly to perceive our true nature, unique beauty, or purpose in life. We become a collage composed of the demands of all these different emotional pressure groups.

THE NEED FOR UNCONDITIONAL LOVE

To break up this collage we have to experience a high degree of that perfect love which casts out all fear. This kind of love usually emanates from the heart of a person who has been broken and then reconstructed. It is shown in their compassion for other broken people. The healed alcoholic who stands before an audience of other alcoholics and says, "My name is David and I am an alcoholic," and then proceeds to tell the story of the hell through which he went, projects a feeling of understanding and compassion to other unhealed alcoholics and is doing much to lead such people to the point of self-acceptance and eventual healing. Alcoholics Anonymous was born because the Christian community was ignoring Christ's requirement that we show unconditional acceptance to the "sinner." There was no place in the church for drunks and derelicts to find help through such tough love. A. A. filled that gap.

As parents it is important for us to communicate to our children that we accept them no matter what they may be guilty of. Thanks to a loving minister, five-year-old Peter found this kind of experience with his father. One Sunday morning Peter took five dollars from a collection plate resting on the communion table. The minister saw him do it and asked him to give back the stolen money; Peter was sure he was going to jail for life. The minister assured him that he would not punish him, but he would tell his father.

"Don't tell daddy," Peter's voice trembled. "He'll kill me."

The minister said he was sure that Peter's fate would be less severe than that. But when he heard about it after the morning service, Peter's father exploded, "I'll kill that kid."

"You mean to tell me you've never stolen anything?" the minister retorted.

The father's eyes took on a distant stare for a moment. Then he replied, "I sure have. When I was just Peter's age, my mother told me to deliver two dozen eggs to a neighbor's house. Only one dozen got there. I told my mother I dropped them. But actually I had sold the whole dozen for about a dime which I kept." Then looking at the minister he said, "Thank you, pastor. I'll talk to Peter this evening."

When the fateful hour came, Peter walked into his father's study expecting the worst. His father took him on his lap and said, "Peter, the pastor told me about your taking the money from the collection plate. When I thought about it, I remembered an experience from my own life when I was just your age."

When his father finished his confession, Peter tearfully looked up and said, "O daddy, I'm so happy. We're both thieves!"

This is the kind of understanding love which leads to self-acceptance and purity.

Theology without compassion is lifeless. Theologians have created scores of theories of the atonement, trying to answer the question, "Why did Jesus Christ die for us?" Often, their learned discussions miss the point; the reason Jesus Christ died for us was that God is love and in Jesus Christ he "who knew no sin" became sin for us.[3] In other words, God so loved us that he entered into our life, not after we had corrected everything, but when everything was wrong. God became "wrong" to show us how we might become right. If we can begin to understand this, we can see that God does not come to us as our judge. He identifies with our failures. He not only shares our guilt, but he accepts the guilt as his own.

The most healing experience a person can have, the

most positive step toward self-acceptance, comes when the truth penetrates our subconscious that Jesus Christ doesn't just forgive our sin—he became our sin. This truth has been heard in revival tents across the country, but when it is experienced within the living rooms of our land, it transforms the whole tenor of the family relationship—the most essential circle of love in our society. When Peter's father came to Peter in penitence instead of judgment, he assumed the role of Christ, thus allowing the little boy to accept himself where he was.

With children of any age, with those whose self-image is diminished by pain or evil, we approach with fear and trembling, and in penitence if possible. When we are unable to do so, it may indicate that our own self-image needs reexamination.

SOME PROBLEMS OF SELF-PROJECTION

Just as we find it hard to forgive others in the areas where we ourselves are weak so, as a rule, we refuse to accept others in the areas where we do not accept ourselves. If we want to find out where our self-image is most in need of repair, we need only pay attention to those around us who most anger us. Then as we seek to accept and bless those people by as many means as possible, our own self-image begins to improve.

Our self-image, not our circumstances, is the primary source of our anxiety. Much energy and money are wasted trying to improve the cosmetics of our psychological image rather than to cut out the cancer of self-condemnation.

June endured her marriage for many miserable

years. She was filled with escapist thoughts. "Oh, if I had a different husband I would be happy. . . . Maybe if my children weren't so much like their father's parents I could cope with them. . . . If I could live in a different house and a better neighborhood, I know there would be less pressure." Her husband's hostilities kept her stomach in knots. She had no pride in her small, unattractive house, and no motivation to improve it. It was only a house—not a home.

Then at a church conference she heard a speaker say: "There is no problem outside yourself. If you are right with yourself on the inside, and in right relationship to yourself, the world around you becomes beautiful and all the people who were once your enemies become your friends."

She heard it explained to the whole group that the healing of old habit patterns and frustrations would not necessarily change overnight, but that as she willed to develop—one step at a time—her unhappy life could unfold gradually into one of beauty and love even when her circumstances remained the same.

Encouraged to take inventory of who and what appeared to rob her of happiness, June began to list all the flaws and faults in others which bothered her. Later, at home alone, she prayerfully asked the Spirit of Christ to reveal to her if these unlovely characteristics were in her. Gradually, she became aware of her slanderous, gossipy tongue, her impatient attitudes, her sloth. Because of her undisciplined life, she realized that the simplest functions of everyday life had become giant obstacles. Her whole life had become an endless obstacle course.

June called her family together and explained her self-discovery. To her amazement, they didn't react contemptuously to her confessions of weakness and inadequacy, but expressed a love and understanding they had never shown her before. When she became totally vulnerable and honest, their response was one of acceptance. There were more moments of frustration. Tempers sometimes flared as the family shared their thoughts and feelings more often and intimately. But her self-acceptance triggered theirs. They tended to blame each other less. Cooperation between children and parents grew. Situations which previously would have caused bickering among the children no longer threatened the peace of the home. The whole atmosphere of the home began to grow more positive.

Month after month, June witnessed a new world unfolding before her eyes. She made the interior of her house lovely if not lavish. Together June and her husband put in shrubbery, a brick patio, and painted the house. It was as though they had to express their inner change in outer improvements.

Upon reflection, June realized that the church conference speaker had been prophetic. Changes in her husband had been insignificant. Her children had not become saints. But by beginning to deal with her internal failures, she found theirs no longer blocked her happiness. Love she could not sense before filled her life. She felt loved and appreciated—something she had never known as a child.

As she told me her story, June agreed that she had become living proof of the truth: improve your own self-acceptance, your internal attitudes, and the external circumstances improve automatically. Acting as if this were true destroys self-pity and creates the will to grow in self-appreciation.

THE SOURCE OF OUR SELF-IMAGE

In order to understand why we function as we do, we must look at the sources of our self-image.

From the moment we become conscious in our mother's womb, immense emotional and spiritual forces emanating from our mother and, to a much lesser degree, our father begin to mold our pliable sensitive emotions which will one day be the adult self. People have tended to ignore the significance of that first nine months in our mother's womb. Every new parent ought to be instructed that what they think and feel is more important in the care of an unborn baby than how they care for themselves physically.

The mother of a two-month-old baby boy had to rush him to the hospital. For no clinically explainable reason he was feverish, dehydrated and starving to death. Intravenous feeding did nothing to stabilize his condition which continued to deteriorate. Visiting in the home of a Christian friend while her son was hospitalized, the mother met a man who, after hearing her story, said, "I think it's important for you to know that I'm a Christian doctor. Christ has shown me the absolute importance of love." Possibly, he informed her, the baby was in its serious condition because it didn't feel loved.

The mother broke into tears. "You're probably right," she said. "I *don't* love the baby and I don't love his father. I never wanted to have the child in the first place and I'm divorcing my husband as soon as I can."

When the doctor asked if he could pray for her, she consented, and with deep tenderness he asked Christ to heal her broken spirit. As he spoke, she felt enveloped in a terrible shroud of bitterness that, over the years of antagonism, she had woven into her marital relationship. She realized she was killing herself with hate because of her own problems and was starving that innocent baby to death in the process.

After the prayer the doctor instructed her to go to the hospital, take her son's face in her hands, look straight into his eyes, calling him by name, and say, "I love you."

When she got to her son's crib in the pediatric ward, she saw her little boy more dead than alive. Suddenly she was filled with a new sense of tender love for him. Reaching down she gently held the baby's face in her hands and told him, "Michael, I love you. O Michael, my baby, I love you."

At that moment the hospital doctor came into the room and asked her what she was doing. She told him the whole story.

He looked straight into her eyes. "I believe everything you say," he told her. "I believe your baby is dying because he has no will to live. What you've just done may possibly save his life."

It did.

The next day the fever broke. The child began to assimilate nourishment and fluids. A week later a loving mother brought her nearly recovered baby son home from the hospital.

A HIDDEN NEED IN THE ADOPTED CHILD

Fortunately, the baby Michael experienced an early reversal from rejection to love and acceptance. With the continuation of that love he is assured a solid foundation for his emotional development. But many people experience anguish beyond infancy because in the womb they were denied love.

A religious leader came to me expressing concern for his second son. The child was eleven years old and keen-minded, but withdrawn and afraid of people. The father asked what he and his wife had done wrong. This was a fallacious assumption that many parents make. And even when it is true, it serves no useful purpose for parents to feel guilty. Most parents give their emotional best to their children. Their guilt feelings, then, should be replaced with the more useful attitude: "I will to improve, but I will not live under any condemnation for giving my best, even if that best was not what it should have been or falls short now of what it can be."

In the case of the withdrawn child's parents, the problem began long before he was theirs. He was adopted at the age of three weeks.

As we saw in Chapter 1, "The Healing Power of Love," many adopted children suffer from the rejection-loneliness pattern. Even when it is adopted a few days after birth, a child harbors in its unconscious mind memories of a mother who abandoned it. The adoptive parents who love such a child will temper and lessen the negative consequences of that early rejection experience. But in many cases inner healing should be attempted to eliminate buried pain.

SUBLIMINAL COMMUNICATION

I suggested to these parents that they speak to their son while he was sleeping. They were told that their son would respond more to this kind of communication. But they were not to speak to him in his bedroom, so that he would not be roused to consciousness. The unconscious mind seems to operate like a shortwave radio. When the conscious mind is still, distant communication is clearly received and understood, and the message penetrates deep into the affective, motivative center of the mind. They were instructed to repeat their son's first, middle, and last name two or three times. Then they were to tell him how deeply loved and accepted he was right then and how blessed he was to come to them through another mother. They were further instructed to add anything else which would reinforce the child's sense of acceptance.

Such subconscious conversation is valuable in many situations where a message of love needs to be sent to the inner child and when the conscious child seems unable to accept that healing communication.

If you choose to use this technique on any child, there are two areas of caution to keep in mind. (1) Don't tell the child how to change its conduct. For instance, don't say, "Tomorrow morning you are going to want to kiss me goodbye before going to school," or, "From now on you will want to wash the supper dishes." This is manipulation. Make your statements emotional and spiritual affirmations only. (2) If more than one person is speaking to the child at different times of the evening, don't vary the message. That can confuse the child. Write out the same message and let all communicating parties repeat the identical message. For those who feel this method is brainwashing, let me hasten to observe that every day the mind is in the slow process of affective conditioning. This is simply a concentrated, purified means of conditioning the deep mind.

I was led to pray for my oldest daughter in a similar way. Lyn at six was experiencing acute pain through her lower body. I took her to our doctor and he prescribed a tranquilizer. When her condition did not improve, I took her to the mental health clinic in our hometown. They gave her a battery of psychological examinations and reported to me that my child was "a very troubled little girl." They recommended therapy, put Lyn on a waiting list, and said they would contact me as soon as there was an opening. My response to this diagnosis was to feel deeply responsible and so guilty.

It was at this time that I was invited to attend my first spiritual life conference. There I experienced a new relationship with Christ. My faith was tremendously deepened.

When I returned home from the conference I was saturated with the love of Christ, and I knew his love could touch my child's mind. Though I had never heard of this method, each night I would stand by Lyn's bed while she was sleeping, and pray. Placing my hand on her head I would silently say, "Jesus, be the bridge between the love Lyn needs and the love I give her." Each night for almost a year I would repeat this silent petition.

The day finally came when I received the long-awaited call from the clinic saying that an opening was available for my daughter. The therapist gave her another series of tests. I knew that Lyn's psychosomatic condition had disappeared months before, but I was not prepared for what was discovered. After studying the new test results, the doctor expressed displeasure that Lyn had been sent to someone else without informing him. The tests, he said, indicated that Lyn was free of the negative emotional symptoms which had caused her problems. When I said that she had had no psychotherapy, he was skeptical. She could not have so measurably improved without it, he said!

Jesus had indeed become the bridge between the love Lyn had needed and the love she received.

Inner healing differs from traditional psychotherapy in its insistence that God is the primary agent of emotional healing. Our role is to cooperate, always knowing that the transcendent, transhuman power of God is at work in us, and in the ill and the disturbed to whom we relate. This does not remove us from our role of responsibility, but it does remove the burden of that responsibility from us, and places it where it belongs—on God.

Inner healing makes available the infinite resources of the Spirit, so that we are not limited to depending on our puny human insights and abilities.

Resorting to prayer becomes an act which allows us to rise to the highest level of healing. It seeks wholeness from the surest source of healing power, in cooperation with that power.

If you are aware that you have a poor self-image but do not know why, there is a specially recommended prayer for you. The prayer is that Jesus will be the bridge between the love you knew in your early, most formative years and the love you should have known. No visualization is necessary for this prayer. It stands on its own. Pray it, believe it, and let God do the work.

"Lord Jesus, may you be the bridge between the love (the person's name) knew and the love they should have known in their relationship with their father and with their mother. Amen."

The prayer can be prayed nightly for oneself or another. For almost a year I offered it each day on my own behalf, and through the exercise new areas of my own emotional need were discovered and healed. To stand in the presence of Jesus Christ and feel his absolute and unconditional love somehow flowing through one's father and mother stimulates our growth toward the kind of self-image and self-acceptance God meant us to have.

A CRISIS IN SEXUALITY

A commonly misunderstood and distorted area of experience is that of the homosexual. The following story traces the diminishing of the male and female self-image with painful clarity.

Without the experience of inner healing, the condition of a prominent husband and wife would have been unredeemed tragedy. The society pages had played up their courtship as "the" romance of the season. The prenuptial parties from rich friends of the two families were followed by an elaborate wedding and a West Indies honeymoon on a yacht.

Both the husband and wife claimed to be dedicated Christians. But both also were deeply confused emotionally. Each had negative and inadequate self-images with extremely unhealthy views of their own sexuality.

Belinda was a masculine, dominant woman. Her mother, her emotional model, was this same aggressive dominant type. Because of this maternal distortion, Belinda knew little of what it meant to be a woman. She was not comfortable unless she was in control. She thought of herself as a liberated woman, but she was enslaved by her need to dominate the male. She did not realize the negative factors behind her attraction to Andrew. He was handsome, rich, and momentarily exciting. But beneath this veneer was a weak, rather passive man who felt the need to be dominated.

Andrew was the product of a millionaire father and a social baroness who was as overcontrolling as Belinda. It is difficult to understand how such a business success as Mr. Phillips could so utterly fail as a father. But he did. He worked hard and played hard, but never with his son. His hobby was expensive machinery for his suburban farm, and the only thing he ever told Andrew about these outrageously expensive toys was "Stay away, don't fool with my equipment."

When I first met Andrew he had been married for five years. His feelings of insecure sexuality were devastating him. Belinda, by this time, was totally "turned off" by her husband. Theirs is a classic example of the too frequent reverse role relationship in marriage: the male dominant woman drawn to a feminine passive man. Some couples stagger through the whole of life in this sorry state. But none find satisfaction or fulfillment in it.

At the outset of their marital crisis the problem seemed to be all Andrew's. The more important problem, that his father had provided him with no adequate model of manhood, expressed itself in a humiliating and unavoidable way. He could not perform sexually after a few months of dissatisfying experiences which became more deliberate, then mechanical and then deteriorated into frustration.

Belinda's complaints about his poor performance further emasculated him. Her heavy-handed control of most phases of their life together made him retreat from her more. At this point her pressure exposed his latent homosexuality. He told me he had turned to men because he found sympathy and compatibility with them. This, however, was not the basic reason.

He found a pattern which stemmed from a mother-minus-father childhood conditioning. He knew how to be feminine better than he knew how to be masculine. This pattern creates much homosexuality.

With the emergence of the gay liberation movement there is some increase in the public's desire to understand the homosexual. This is good. But most of the positive response to the gay subculture is more sympathy than understanding. This is as true of the heterosexual as of the homosexual segment of society. The callous attitude, "Homosexuality is sinful, *period*," is so medieval as to deserve only the passing comment that such an attitude can only intensify the homosexual's burden. It offers nothing of the love and enlightenment which can help the gay person find a whole and happy life.

What should be understood is that many homosexuals are expressing arrested emotional development. Few homosexuals from birth have experienced the anomalous glandular condition which determines a borderline male-female body and emotional response. The subject of this rare type of physiological homosexual condition deserves special treatment and is not included in this discussion. Andrew, like most bisexuals, was not one of these.

Everyone has some immaturity. And immaturity in an adult is also arrested emotional development. It may be more socially acceptable for a man to be a woman-chaser than a homosexual, but in reality he is only one step away from a gay mentality. Both are rooted in an insecure male self-image. The opposite expression of this condition, the lesbian, is one who never found a feminine model in her mother. What the "stud," the sex-queen, and the homosexual need is maturity at the point of their arrested development, not condemnation.

Protesting homosexuals may miss the point of their problem by wanting to be accepted as different but normal. The truth is, their sexual pattern is inadequate. If it is evil, it is only so because of how they use it. If they choose to exploit persons for their own gratification and to ignore their own need to grow emotionally and spiritually that attitude is wrong, but hardly limited to the homosexual world. Exploitation is equally plaguing in heterosexual immaturity.

RECONSTRUCTING A SELF-IMAGE

Like many homosexuals, Andrew never had an adequate opportunity to relate to, and subconsciously identify with, a mature parent figure of his own sex. This is the primary cause. The cure is to make that bridge, to fill that void, to bring to the inner child the experience of identifying with the parent of their sex. This allows the process of sex identity, arrested in childhood, to revive and develop properly.

When Andrew told me that his father had never spent any time with him, I said, "All right, we are going to spend an hour in guided prayer. You are going to spend a day with your daddy. You can do anything you ever wanted to do with him."

"But Ruth," he protested, "I can't conceive of him giving me a minute, let alone a day."

"Where did he spend all of his time?"

"Working on his damned machinery."

I asked him to close his eyes and picture himself as a teenage boy back home.

"Go out there and help him work on the tractor."

"Ruth, he won't even let me come into the barn."

The child within this man felt totally rejected by his father. How arrogant it is to hate, judge, or condemn a man whose homosexuality is simply an expression of his need for his father's love.

"All right," I said, "let Jesus move toward your father, and see Jesus in his perfect, strong, yet tender masculine nature blessing your father."

Slowly, with much inward struggle, a positive image of "father" began to emerge. This critical point may take weeks of deliberate prayer and constructive homework with the imagination. But Andrew was able to proceed in about one half hour.

"What is your daddy saying to you?" I finally asked.

"He says he needs a screwdriver."

"Well, go get it."

He was silent as he imagined himself going to the tool box.

"What did he say when you gave it to him?"

"He said I brought him the wrong kind." There were still vestiges of the old rejecting image.

"Let him describe the right kind of screwdriver. Describe it aloud."

At that moment I heard Andrew saying, "Son, the kind of screwdriver I want is a Phillips. Now, I know you don't know what that is, but its tip is star-shaped and the screw looks like this."

A smile came to Andrew's face. One more important step had been taken toward uniting a father with his son. They soon got the tractor fixed. Andrew said, "Daddy says he needs to get some parts for the tractor in town."

The next imaginary event was unexpected by me. But to this man recalling his childhood it was natural to hear his father say, "We're going to town in the pickup truck, son. Go get some hot dogs and buns. We'll cook them in the woods." After some frustration Andrew pictured himself bringing the food out to the truck. He then envisioned himself climbing into the cab next to his dad. He was proud as punch as he sensed his daddy looking at him with pride and thanking him for making the hot dogs just right.

It was a simple incident to visualize, but through it the Spirit was healing Andrew's early feelings of rejection. Evidently, the little child felt he did everything wrong. But now when his daddy thanked him for a job well done, even a job that leaned more in the direction of mother (preparing a meal) than father, it was a bridge, the kind of small step of which there must be many, to male acceptance and the establishment of an adequate male self-image.

This experience of doing something for his father in mother's domain, the kitchen, has a subtle quality of compassionate understanding which deserves special consideration. A male homosexual might find it an obstacle of the first magnitude to step right into the father's world. But if, even in imagination, the father came into his and led him out, the transition is much more likely.

This was the approach used by Jesus when he asked Simon Peter, "Simon, son of John, do you love me?" The problem, in Peter's case, was not homosexuality. But it was love. Twice Jesus asked the question, "Do you love me?" and Simon replied, "You know I *like* you." He could not rise to the level of the love Jesus knew. So, in compassion and sympathy Jesus said finally, "Simon, son of John, do you *like* me?"[4] That is an essential element in growth toward a proper self-image. The significant persons who are attempting to correct the image of another must adapt their understanding to that of the broken person. This was achieved to a high degree in Andrew's case as he moved, ever so carefully, toward true manhood.

After we finished the guided prayer, I instructed Andrew to read a Scripture each day on the subject of Jesus' healing of the sick. And every time he said the word "Jesus," he was to call him "Daddy." This was for the purpose of reinforcing Andrew's emerging father-image.

For more than a year Andrew made a concentrated inward effort to build his new father relationship. And, predictably, on the spiritual side of the ledger, Jesus Christ, the Son of *man* became more real. Andrew became active in the couple's group in his local church. From time to time he received further counseling from a spiritually sensitive psychiatrist. I received a number of long-distance phone calls from him, and we went through a number of guided meditations to help strengthen his growing father approval. As Andrew's self-image improved, he lost interest in male sexual relationships completely. And as his normal responses to the feminine developed, they became more spontaneous, virile, and fulfilling.

Andrew's story does not end on a "lived happily ever after" note. Belinda is just beginning to face her equally difficult problems. But she is making some progress as she relates to a man named Andrew, whose self-image of manhood is now adequate because it draws its strength from the Son of man.

KEEPING EYES ON THE GOAL

Reference was made earlier about how to get a clearer view of the shadowed side of our self-image. By noting the type of people who anger us, we get strong clues to our own weakness. But the man who is struggling with his self-image, or the woman who is having an identity crisis, needs to take affirmative action.

One effective image-altering tool is a "positive portrait list." Starting with a prayer for guidance, take paper and pen and develop a list of qualities and characteristics you would like to find both in your inner life and in your outer relationships. Aim as high as you feel you can. Then each morning and night read the list aloud; affirm it. Don't try to live up to the ideal, just ponder it. This morning and evening review should continue for at least one year. Such a discipline takes little effort, just faithful persistence.

As time goes by, you may want to review your ideal portrait with an eye to altering and improving it. But stick to your original sketch for a few weeks at least. Such concentrated consideration will always realize a better self-image. For those who trust God, no needed positive improvement is impossible. The promise is given to all, "Behold I am the Lord, the God of all flesh; is anything too hard for me?"[5]

7.

The Healing Power of
RELEASE

When we face areas of our life which are not as they ought to be, when we experience ugliness in situations which seem to defy correction, sometimes the last thing we should do is "try harder." What we may need is an experience of release. The key to growth is to abandon our efforts and to desire to embrace the grace of God.

RELEASE OF THE TRAGIC

Sometimes guilt causes us to cling to the tragic and painful, holding it to our hearts. We must learn to release to God all guilty images and all tragic memories in our past. When we do, a chain reaction of blessing and healing can take place.

Diane had lost her beautiful eighteen-year-old son, Tommy. In a state of deep depression, he had taken his own life. In the days that followed, Diane had to lean heavily on the grace of God. Many marveled at her strength and beauty of spirit. Then one day in a moment of weakness, guilt over her son's death overwhelmed her and she attempted to take her life with an overdose of sleeping pills. It was a close call, but Diane lived. After recovery, she went into psychotherapy sessions in an effort to deal with her guilt. The more she concentrated on it the more she relived it, and the worse it got. She felt she wasn't trying hard enough, but the harder she tried the more monumental the guilt seemed.

One day while sitting alone at home, she began to ask God to forgive her for how she failed her son and God. As she did, she imagined Jesus walking up to her with her son beside him. They were holding hands.

"Release him to me," she heard Jesus whisper. "Give him to me completely." With every cell of her being, she responded, "He's yours. I give him to you, Jesus."

Some time later at a conference, a young man next to Diane broke into tears in response to a prayer offered for the emotionally suffering. His pain was so great he collapsed sobbing into her arms. As she held the young stranger, she heard the inner voice say, "Diane, this is your son you're holding. And this is the way you are going to have him from now on— in other young men who need your mother's heart."

As the words flooded Diane's mind, she began to rock rhythmically back and forth as she had done with Tommy so many times. The young stranger's pain and tears began to fade.

Diane's new experience prodded her to search for reasons why her guilt had cut off realization of God's love. As she reflected upon her past, she realized she had loved her father and her only son Tommy more than Jesus. She had idolized them. They were untouchable, beyond her emotional reach. Through faith-imagination exercises she visualized both her father and son on pedestals. Then she visualized her father stepping down off the pedestal and embracing her. And then Tommy. At last she was able to imagine Jesus walking up to her. With new comprehension, with no reluctance, she at last could walk into the arms of her Lord and Savior.

As is so often the case in the process of inner healing there is another link in this chain of blessing. Diane and her husband began a new relationship, able to share in ways they had never guessed possible. No implications of fault are intended against Diane's psychotherapist. It is possible that he prepared her consciousness for the inner healing that followed. Psychotherapy and inner healing are made for each other, and should be wedded. Diane has recognized that her problems intensified as she focused upon them; it wasn't until she released them that her agony released her. Release gave birth to joy—in a new relationship with her husband, a new ministry as mother to others, and a new world of beauty revolving around its true center—the Son. She contagiously shares it with others. Hers is a story of release which can heal the heartbroken every time.

RELEASE FOR PHYSICAL HEALING

We have seen in our chapter on surrender that the surrendered Christian knows that he cannot heal, and in the chapter on faith, that his faith must center in the divine healer. Further, it should be understood that when we are called to pray for the healing of another, we must release the situation, the ailment, the prayer target, to God.

It is an error to pray for the sick with the reservation, "If it be thy will." A God of total love wills all of his children to know wholeness. Jesus healed all who came to him. When a person is not healed, it is not because God will not; it is that God cannot *under certain circumstances.* Failure to realize healing is like failure to have the light go on when you turn the wall switch to "on." We don't waste time wondering whether God wanted the light on. We simply check the bulb. If necessary, we further check the socket, the wiring, the switch, the fuse box, and the outside power source. If all are in order, the light *will* go on. So it is with healing. God wills everyone well; but we have to meet his conditions.

When healing does not occur, one of the vital points to check is release. Have we released the sick or injured person to the Father God? When that release has not taken place, the anxiety acts like improper wiring. The power cannot flow from God to the object of our healing prayer. Agnes Sanford, one of the pioneers of the healing ministry in the major denominational churches, said that you can't do two hundred and twenty volts worth of work with a one hundred and ten volt current. When more power is needed to heal the sick, it is up to us to find that greater flow before the healing can be achieved. Often the act of release allows the power to flow as it was meant to flow.

As with physical healing, much inner healing is a product of release. The mind cannot be reconstructed as long as one clings to self-control. "The eternal God is your refuge," says the Bible, "and underneath are the everlasting arms."[1] But God's healing embrace is never felt by the struggling. Sometimes it is difficult to let go and let God. But it is not nearly so difficult as being chained to the pain of past guilt, as was Diane, or to a crippling accident, or to "terminal" cancer. When we release ourselves and our situation to the Spirit, we are a step nearer to being held and healed in the everlasting arms.

RELEASING OUR CHILDREN

Another area where release is essential is in the raising of children. It is a common mistake to cling to our children when we should give them over to God. The asthmatic child, for instance, may be an easily detected product of a parent who could not let go. Many psychosomatic diseases are the product of "smother love." But there are more subtle sicknesses of soul which afflict both the child and parent when parents don't learn to let go.

Parents need to care but cannot afford to cling. A baby, secure in its mother's womb, would die if kept there. The wisdom of God takes care of that first necessary separation at birth. But that umbilical cord can symbolically reach into and poison adult relationships. Does a mother cut the umbilical cord of her control and concern when her child leaves for kindergarten? becomes a teenager? leaves for college? enters marriage? The act of release *in varying degrees* can be just as essential at each one of these stages of emotional restructuring.

As parents we must discover that sensitivity which releases but does not abandon. A child should sense that he or she is free to fly, to use the wings of maturity as much as possible. But we must let our children know that the parental nest of love and understanding is still theirs to use whenever they feel they must return. We must be careful not to bend them to our sympathies when they need only our encouragement to grow. But we must always affirm to them our love, our faith in them, our available helping hand.

I can remember experiencing a moment which was at the same time deeply painful and one of my proudest maternal victories. When my son left home to go to college in Syracuse, New York, he experienced severe cultural shock. For one thing, he moved from a high school where he was popular and successful to the relative obscurity of a large university. All the old familiar roots had been dug up, and his new independence left him confused.

On our first trip to see him, he shared the pain and the struggles caused by his move and his quest for maturity. His final remarks on the subject were, "Mother and Daddy, I have finally come to the place in my mind that if you two died and I were left alone, it would now be okay."

My big, attractive, 6'2" son had become a man. Earlier I had released him; I had willed that he be pushed out of the nest. Now the goal was realized. And mama was nearly devastated by the victory!

My release in this separation process began three years earlier. I was preparing to go away for a weekend retreat when Scotty came in and sat on my bed while I packed.

"Are you going to be away all weekend?" he asked.

"Yes, all weekend."

"Well, I'm sure our trips are certainly going to be different," he said. "I just hope you have as good a time as I'm going to. All of our gang are going to the beach at Ocean Drive. We're chipping in our money to buy all the booze we can, and we're planning a contest to see who can drink the most."

What an inspiring filial send-off to a religious retreat! I had spent untold hours praying for my children. All of my children are different, but Scotty had a special energy which spilled constantly into unexpected and surprising areas. He also seemed to be more rebellious than the others. Still I was unprepared for his announcement about a drunken weekend. How could he do such a thing to me, I thought, when I was going on this spiritual weekend? Although I had determined to be above succumbing to family problems, there I was—seething with anger toward Scotty. But I was smart enough to know I could not discipline a tall, broad-shouldered son.

Without saying anything, I began to pray, putting Scotty in God's hands. And God began to put something in my mind I could hardly believe. The thought came, "Give him five dollars more."

God has lost his mind, was my reaction, if this is what he is telling me! But I knew this thought had to have come from God—I would never have thought of such a thing.

I took the money and went into Scotty's room. "Honey," I said to him, "just to be sure you have a good time, here is five dollars more." I thought I was going to have to pick his big frame up off the floor. Braced for a lecture—he got a donation.

When we truly release uncontrollable situations to God, it requires a faith that God will order events to bring a solution. Often there is the temptation to take the problem back. But when we trust enough to release a child to God and hold to that release, we need only "stand still and see the victory of the Lord."[2]

When I went away that weekend I released the problem of my son and alcohol to God's care. He was the only one big enough to handle it.

Upon my return on Sunday afternoon, Scotty greeted me with, "Well, I guess Dad told you about my weekend."

"No, honey, he didn't. I forgot to ask about it when he picked me up at the airport." I realized I had forgotten about it during the whole weekend.

"Well, I guess it's going to make you real happy to hear this. When we got down there Friday night, I chipped in my money and got my share of the booze. I tried my best to enjoy it, but it turned out to be the most miserable night of my life. I got sick. I got so sick, I actually prayed. I asked God if he'd just let me live until morning, I'd get home as fast as I could. So I sold my share on Saturday morning and hitchhiked home. I was home in bed by 10:00 A.M."

It must be made clear that Scotty was to face many more crises, and has experienced times of unhappiness since then. But each event has been a new challenge to me to release him to the only power able to raise him—and by "raise," I mean raise him to God.

Releasing love always wins. But it can be painful. It is much easier to try to stay in control than to let go. But when we refuse to release, we end up by playing God. And such a role is at best ridiculous and at worst tragic.

It is sometimes hard to remember that our heavenly Father is God, that he has the power and wisdom to save our sanity and our children's integrity. The direct result of a young person's being released by the parents is that he or she, no longer controlled and manipulated, can begin to come into his or her own. When we release our children, they are freed to develop necessary qualities for emotional stability: decision making, learning through failure, and the acceptance of responsibility. They are also free to learn that they need God more than parents for guidance.

DIFFERENCES IN PARENTAL RELEASE

Each child in a family needs a different disciplinary pattern and guidance. The sensitive child may take less talking to and develop a later independence of parental control. Another child may need a firm disciplinary hand and a release in early adolescence from parent dependency. There is no way precision guidance can be given to parents on how to replace the tension of overcontrol by release. And it would be unfair to take my experience with my son as an example of how every parent should cut the cords which bind them to their children.

Many parents need only understand the principle of release to apply it. Frequently such ready application indicates that their parents did not overcontrol them. That was the case in my life. If anything, I was given a larger degree of freedom from parental demands than most children, and that has made it easier for me to let go.

DILEMMA OF THE WESTERN WORLD

In some cases a mother may find it especially hard to release the children. This is often the case when a husband is not significantly involved in the discipline of the children, and she is concerned to protect and bless them. Many mothers who have a normal attachment to their children feel an unusual and consequently unhealthy degree of responsibility for their care and nurture. God intended the teenager to experience a major release from mother at the age of puberty. This independence cannot evolve properly however, unless the husband is ready and able to take on his role in the emotional development and discipline of the children.

The problem of the masculine dominant mother and the feminine passive father is endemic in our society. Adults who have suffered from a lack of release on the part of the mother and a lack of responsibility on the part of the father will tend to replay the role of the parent as they have learned it. Strong aggressive mothers tend to develop daughters who are strong, aggressive wives and mothers. Fathers who are only involved in decision making, and in the discipline of the children, tend to create sons and fathers after their own weak images.

In our Western industrial society, the home has suffered terribly from the bigamous demand that men be wed to their jobs. The business world has created an atmosphere of "total commitment to the company" which is in conflict with the natural pattern of emotional and physical involvement at home. The problem, however, is far less severe and oppressive now. Technological efficiency and workers' rights give men much more opportunity to be home if they wish. But because generations of their fathers and grandfathers before them have been conditioned to to be away from home, the opportunity often is rejected. Men unconsciously prefer to spend their time "with the boys," bowling, golfing, sporting or just keeping busy away from the family circle.

The Holy Spirit is breaking this vicious cycle. But it is demanding major healing of the hearts of parents and children.

METHODS FOR BREAKING THE OVERCONTROLLING PATTERN

Mothers who awaken to their overcontrolling patterns often have to do three things to find release.

1. Visualizing Release

They find it necessary to actualize release through visualization. That is, they have to picture the act of cutting the emotional umbilical cord between themselves and the dominated adolescent. The mother can do this by imagining the child standing before her with the cords connecting her body to her child's. Usually they are umbilical to umbilical, heart to heart, or head to head. Asking Jesus to come into this scene, she visualizes him handing her a sword. With it she cuts the cords which bind her to her child. This imagined action confirms the act of release in an emotionally decisive way. Many mothers who have said to me that they already felt they had given their anxiety about their children to God have found it traumatic to go through this visualized release. Others who could not give their children up to God by trying harder have succeeded by cutting the unhealthy ties in this manner.

2. Reconstructing the Image of Motherhood

In order to maintain the attitude of release, a large percentage of mothers counseled have had to go back to their youth to reconstruct the image of their mother, or they too easily revert back to the old overcontrolling patterns learned from her. This is a more demanding process which begins with the recognition that only God can achieve such a memory transformation. In that same attitude, the woman must ask the Spirit to perfect her feminine image. For those who see Mary the mother of Jesus as the ultimate mother figure, she is the ideal model. I would agree with a critic who might object that an intangible, invisible personage such as Mary is hardly substantive enough to act as a model for the subconscious. I only know that women who have asked the Spirit of Truth to teach them of womanhood through the spirit of Mary have felt an enhancement, sometimes even a transformation, of their womanhood. This has enabled them to express a more authentic, rich femininity in their relationships and lessens their tendency to dominate their children or husbands.

3. Involving the Father

The final factor concerns the need to bring the husband back to his proper role in the home. It is of little benefit for a mother to withdraw her masculine dominance if the husband continues to be passive or incompetent in relating to his children. The first tendency of a woman who is awakening to her proper role is to want an immediate, comparable change in her husband. This seldom occurs. The usual result of the wife's changing perspective and consequent actions is confusion on the part of the man and an emotional void in the home which is difficult for everyone. It is at this moment that the wife's inner life, her faith, her will to hold to an unrealized vision, will make the difference. Pressure from the wife to force change in her husband will make the uncertain man even more uncertain of his manhood. He will tend to fight back or will retreat more into his world away from home. But if the wife can hold to the image of her husband as strong, if she is willing to spend a few minutes each day in a relaxed state visualizing a husband who is warm, responsive and Christlike, her faith-imagination will carry the day.

It may seem unfair to emphasize the woman's role over the man's in this reconstruction of the male-female role relationship. But in a vast majority of cases the woman is the first to recognize that something is wrong in the home. She is where the action is. The children are tied to her apron strings. This tends to motivate her to seek help before the husband. It is not that the husband is more callous. It is, rather, that his world has been constructed away from home. And it is easier for him to ignore the real problem through readily accessible escapes. Of course, when the husband and wife are working together to reverse this improper role-relationship, the change is more rapid and occurs with greater ease. Where there is the exception and the husband sees the need to discover an enlightened manhood and fatherhood, he can follow the same steps, beginning with release, using Jesus as the model of manhood.

BEING FREED FROM AN OVERCONTROLLING RELATIONSHIP

The effects of overcontrol are destructive wherever the tentacles reach.

A divorcée came to me suffering from much anxiety. She had left her husband because she had been unable to cope with his violent dictatorial attitude. His oppressive demands and control over her had made her feel she was losing her own identity completely. But even after the separation, the bondage to him continued. At night she was plagued with what she felt were his projected thoughts.

My first reaction was that the woman was trying to excuse her own incompetence. I thought it patent nonsense. But as she described her feelings, I sensed that there was more substance to her suggestion than I had first thought. Suggesting that we use faith-imagination in prayer, I told her to visualize her ex-husband standing before her.

"Any parts of your body you feel that he has control of, visualize a cord attached from that part of his body to yours."

As she began the process, there formed in her mind the image of cords running from his head to hers, from his hands, heart, and feet to hers. Eventually she said, "I feel that the ropes are all around my neck and chest strangling me."

I had her imagine Jesus with a sword standing beside her and her former husband. The sword symbolizes many things—the Spirit, love, man's active generative power. Here it symbolized the power of God to loose from bondage.

"In his love and desire for your release, see him raise the sword and cut every cord binding you to your husband."

Immediately the woman fell forward in the chair in a semi-conscious state! Laying her carefully on the floor, I prayed, asking Jesus to bless and heal her ex-husband. Then I asked him to remove every scar created by their pain-filled relationship.

As she opened her eyes, her first words were, "I'm free! I'm free!" More significantly, the feeling of control from the ex-husband was broken.

It should be noted that even if the woman's condition was imaginary rather than objective, the process successfully dealt with the problem. Rarely do we have a precise and accurate picture of our actual emotional problems. But love is able to deal with fantasies as well as factual ills. The pain, real or imaginary, can be eliminated, thus allowing the sufferer to be free to live more fully.

BEING FREED FROM THE NEED TO CONTROL

I experienced the opposite side of the overcontrolling coin some time ago. A close friend and I had made an agreement to call each other when we needed a helping hand. We were both busy, fairly secure—but both sensed a desperate need for a friend. We agreed that social situations would not count—that this was a special "friend-in-need" pact.

Soon after that I frantically called her house. When I found that she was not there, I left a message which I knew she would interpret correctly: "Help!"

Fifteen minutes later she called back. She was at the beauty parlor and her hair was soapy with shampoo. When she heard the note of anguish in my voice she said, "If you don't mind soap in my hair, I'll be right there."

I told her to finish, the emergency was not that dire, but to come as soon as possible.

Within the hour I heard her running up the steps. When I opened the door she embraced me and said, "Ruth, what's the matter? What can I do to help?"

"I don't know," I said. "I just don't know. I feel totally frustrated and for no reason."

I began to pour out to her all of the things on my mind. I was wondering how long it was going to be before Scotty got into medical school. I shared my concern over a dear friend who was ill and was not improving. And I began to catalog my other anxieties from an overloaded schedule to exhausting personal demands.

"Ruth," she said suddenly, "you've lost control! There is nothing you can do about any of these situations."

So that was it! Trying to control and being unable to causes frustration. Being the one controlled causes frustration, and in our frustration we immediately react by trying to control another. My every problem was centered in circumstances beyond my control. What deadly poisonous impulse in me, what unidentified monster within my subconscious compelled me to desire control? Not only over situations—but persons!

My friend prayed for me, asking God to help me release Scotty, my sick friend, my schedule, my future, and every other person and situation I was holding on to.

"Jesus, help Ruth to give all these loved ones and their lives back into your care. Help her to release them and let go."

And the release came. I experienced a new measure of deep inner peace. More important, I began to see that manipulative overconcern produces bondage in the other person. It is possible to control others in ways they do not suspect. I have since learned that many are in bondage to other members of their family in this way. They sometimes feel they have no life of their own. Such unconscious control may deprive another of a feeling of self-identity, or prevent growth or healing.

RELEASE AND MEEKNESS

The will to overcontrol and its consequences lie at the root of many psychosomatic diseases, from asthma to multiple sclerosis according to some doctors of psychosomatic medicine. The evidence is growing to support this claim. And much hostility and violence which threaten to destroy the fabric of civilized society also can be traced to this same ugly characteristic.

By contrast, the loving, releasing spirit is the mortar which holds life together. This kind of person I believe to be what Jesus called "the meek." I had always thought of the meek as being those who had an attitude of mind which made them "teachable." And this is in part correct. But from the perspective of inner healing, meekness is the ability to act without either the desire to control or fear of those who seek to control us. How much this world needs the meek, those who will release others to be themselves, who will release situations from manipulative ego trips, and release themselves and others from the stress and tension that causes dis-ease.

Jesus taught the principle of release in the Beatitudes when he said, "Blessed are the meek, for they shall inherit the earth."[3] He also revealed in that statement that release does not mean abandoning one's rights as an individual. Meekness as the product of release should never connote a milquetoasty lack of self-respect or a denial of our personal rights. The opposite is true. When we release others to God's wisdom, we participate in one of the higher forms of prayer.

In the Greek language of the New Testament, the word translated *meek* means teachableness, not weakness. It is the characteristic which describes that of a wild horse that has been broken and come under the control of a bridle. Its energies now are usable. There is a carefree beauty in a stallion running wild on the range. But that isn't to be compared with the magnificence of a horse and its rider, moving as one, to achieve a higher goal than the horse alone could ever know. When we come under the dominion of God's guidance, we are free to release others to be either the wild stallion or the Lippizaner show horse with the Holy Spirit as rider.

My early conditioning led me to believe that to be a servant of Christ was to be a desolate underdog. I no longer believe that. I know that the meek who have released others to be themselves, free of manipulation, will indeed inherit the earth.

RELEASE IN A MARRIAGE

One of the most difficult areas in which to practice release is a marriage. In Sally and Joel's relationship the emotional problems were extremely complex.

Sally came to my study convinced that she was an utter failure as a woman. Physically she could not have been more feminine. She had the subtle loveliness of wealth and beauty owned without ostentation. Her gold blond hair was casually coiffed. Her make-up enhanced her classic features. And her powder blue and white original was tasteful without studied elegance. But her eyes were utterly poverty-stricken with pain and sadness.

"I'm glad you've come," I said to her. Before she could speak our eyes met and she burst into tears. I reached over and took her hand and waited for her to relieve enough pent-up emotion to share her story.

After some minutes she calmed and began to speak. "I don't know what to tell you. I've done everything I know how to do to make it with my husband. I know I've made mistakes. Some were bad mistakes; I had two affairs. But it was out of sheer boredom and frustration, and both experiences were only momentarily satisfying. Then I was devastated with guilt. After all Christ had done for me, Ruth, I don't know why I have done such a thing."

"Many Christians have run into the same problem, Sally," I answered. "You don't need to feel like a Judas. It's an ironic truth that often your heart is more vulnerable, less repressed, and thus more open to such unfortunate conduct after you've experienced Christ's love. You are more likely to allow deep needs and hurts to surface once you sense within that Christ will never abandon you, no matter what you feel or do. Sometimes affairs are the product of the fact that after you have tasted Christ's love you became more aware of your need for love."

"Well," she responded, "it didn't make me love men more. I came to feel I hated all of them, and I was eaten up with guilt. Both of the men I got involved with were members of my church. I guess I thought if they were religious it would make my infidelity okay. But it was so grim, finally, that I was ready to give up my faith. I felt so unworthy to be a Christian.

"That's when some of the young women of the church began talking to me about a course they said they were taking which had helped a lot of women in their marriages. So, I enrolled in it. And to tell you the truth, it seemed to make quite a difference. I was given a book which promised to improve my femininity. I was told that by practicing such disciplines as greeting my husband with a kiss when he comes in the door, being more sensual in dress and conjugal activities, my marriage would flower. My husband, Joel, started to pay more attention to me. He even began to be a little romantic.

"But then something went wrong. One night he came home from the office and I greeted him in my loveliest organdy gown, all primped and perfumed, and he treated me like trash. Well, I blew up, and told him I hated him and wished I could die. And I meant both. I've tried a few more times to be a ravishing wife, but every time he touches me I feel dead all over. Ruth, I'm just ready to give up." She began to cry again.

"I know you're hurting, but it's important that I ask you one question. Do you want your marriage healed no matter what the cost may be? Or—have you come to me for more temporary relief?"

"I couldn't be more miserable than I already am. I'll try anything."

"Sally, the first thing I want to say to you is that these marriage courses sometimes work—for the short term. A few women who have simply been careless and have no essential antagonism toward the male will experience the promised improvements. But most women discover that after the reconstructed honeymoon is over their plight is even more desperate. Your intentions were right but you never understood your real problem. Good make-up doesn't make a corpse come alive. It just makes it a little easier to look at. I think you were trying to be a good mortician, when what you needed was for Christ to bring to life a part of you that has been dead for years."

Sally said she didn't understand what I meant. So I told her that often our uncontrollable negative reactions are the product of early childhood experiences and that no amount of high resolution can create a lasting, positive change. It only temporarily creates a bearable surface improvement. Then I asked her, "How did you relate to your father?"

"There wasn't much relating," she replied, "because he was never around, or at least, it seemed that way to me. When I was very young, Mother tells me, Daddy was so busy getting his business going he was never at home. But when I was in high school he had three department stores he loved, two sets of golf clubs he loved, and a family he put up with on some weekends."

"Your husband is not your problem, Sally. I think you just described your problem."

"You're confusing me," she said. "What does Daddy's empire building have to do with my marriage? Joel's just a busy surgeon."

"Yes," I answered, "Joel may not be a carbon copy of your father, but he is a reasonable facsimile at the critical point of your problem. Joel often is too busy for you. And that touches the nerve of rejection exposed in your relationship with your father. You expect the significant man of your life to reject you, to have no time for you. So while you were playing happy-housewife with Joel, you were sure on the level of your deep mind that he would treat you 'like trash'—to use your expression. In other words, your heart was sending Joel a double message, a love-hate message. You were saying, 'I want to get closer because I want your love, but I don't want to get closer because I know you are going to turn your back on me.' That makes him feel confused. This probably causes him to feel like a failure as a lover and husband and this, consequently, drives him more and more into his own world, the world of medicine and golf where he feels relaxed and successful."

SUBMISSION AND SURRENDER VERSUS RELEASE

"Yes, I see," Sally said glumly, "but it sounds like you're telling me that because my father did what he did, I'll never make it in my marriage with Joel."

"Not at all," I corrected. "I was saying you'll never make it unless you allow the Spirit to remove your unhealthy image of your father and reconstruct a new one, one of a warm, responsible, attentive father. But before you can do that, you must release Joel."

"You mean let him leave me?"

I told her I wasn't talking about physical release, though it could come to that. What I was referring to was her attitude.

"The first thing you should release is your attitude that Joel is to blame."

"But I didn't think that Joel was to blame. I tried that; it didn't work. And the school taught me that I should surrender my life to Joel, that I should submit to him at all times. When I obeyed what they said, he treated me like trash."

"We're talking about three very different areas, Sally: submission, surrender, and release. Submission and surrender take place only between you and Christ, not between you and any other human. You've surrendered your life and your attitudes to Christ. You've submitted to some of his disciplines. There are other disciplines for you to learn about and to practice. Like most of us, there have been some that you have neglected—and violated . . ."

"I'll never go that way again," she interrupted. "But

doesn't the Bible say, 'Wives, submit to your husbands'?"

"There are schools that translate scripture that way. And many qualifications and much argument pro and con. The more acceptable translation is 'be accountable'—in the same way that he should be accountable to you, but not in the same way that you both should be accountable to Christ. There are many differences between your loyalties and duties to Joel as contrasted with those due to Christ. A general surrenders his army, a sheriff surrenders his prisoner and gives up all dominion to another. In the same way you surrender to Christ and are converted to his uses, purposes, love, and power. You submit to his rule.

"You do release another. You release him to be what Christ wants him to be according to Christ's timetable and design. You release others, you release situations; you do not surrender to them. You surrender your own attitudes and impulses to Christ. You release the attitudes, impulses, and actions of one such as Joel. Perhaps the most important thing you release about others is your ideas about how they should be— or how they should act."

Sally's first step toward inner healing was to join me in a prayer where she released Joel to be Joel— regardless of the costs to her. Her second step was to release his side of their marriage relationship, and to surrender hers to Christ. By her third visit she understood that for Joel to be himself did not require her to stay with the situation. Now she was free to follow Christ and not to be her own or Joel's dictator.

At last she was ready for unfamiliar exercises in faith-imagination. In her imagination she projected herself back to her childhood. She saw her father blessed by Jesus, giving and receiving love in the family, becoming a loving and caring person.

With new visions of her father's love came Sally's sense of the inadequacy of her own self-image. Key ugly incidents of her past were dealt with by Jesus, and healed. As her realization of his love flowed into her consciousness, as forgiveness enriched blighted past relationships, Sally realized that she was a new person, with a sense of self-worth that grew to the stature of mature womanhood less dependent upon Joel, more dependent upon Jesus.

As her self-image improved, her outrage increased with each recollection of the school that had tried to teach her to be someone else. She referred to it as "those morticians."

"Ruth," she said, "they told me that they were trying to liberate the forces within my own personality to allow me to find my true self. The 'forces' they were trying to liberate had already been liberated—or rather let out of their cage—twice. These were the forces that were uncontrolled because they were directed by my negative self-image."

Sally continued her inner-healing exercises with me until she recognized that her relationship to Joel was not dependent upon anything he did, that she was responsible for how she reacted and that this was dependent upon the quality of her own self-image.

At our last session I suggested that issues in any marriage were inevitably complicated by what the ego demanded from one's spouse. There always is the question of what one wants. And the decisive factor in her relationship with Joel was that her new needs sprang from a new mature self-image rather than from the inadequate, impoverished image that she had before she began her inner healing. She knew that Joel was not her problem, that she could not expect him to change. She knew that release was primary, and kept saying, "If Joel never changes, I will accept him and release him into God's hands." I then made it clear that she must repeatedly affirm, "By the grace of God *I* will to change."

"But if Joel never changes" she said, "what's the use of all the sacrifice and struggle?"

"Do you think it's sacrifice to find a new sense of wholeness and maturity? God isn't going to lead you to a dead-end. From the moment you give up the struggle and let Christ do what he alone can, you will be entering a more fulfilling experience of life within. Joel and the other outer circumstances won't any longer dictate whether you are up or down. You will find it tempting to blame Joel again. But as you repeatedly refuse to hold on to this immature attitude, your growth in happiness is assured."

She confessed that it made her weak in the knees to face the prospect of living on with Joel's cold indifference. Yet she had no other alternative, she felt, than to release the whole "hopeless mess" over to God.

The months that followed were not storybook perfect. Twice she phoned me in utter despair. But each time she had the wisdom to release the situation again.

About a year and a half after Sally first released her marriage to God, I was seated in a restaurant lunching with Sally and a young military officer's wife. After Sally's friend had told us of her deteriorating marriage and about an affair she had been having, Sally looked over at me with a smile on her face. Then turning to the despairing wife she said, "Well, your marriage couldn't be any more hopeless than mine was. And I only hope you and Sid can become as happy as Joel and I are. I think Ruth has something to tell you."

I turned to her, looked her full in the face, smiled, and said very deliberately "Sally, what do *you* have to say?"

8.

The Healing Power of
PURPOSE

When my father James Earl Carter died, part of
my mother died with him. They had lived a long,
full life together and when he was gone, she was
left with a dark void of restlessness, frustration, and
lack of joy. She tried to find fulfillment in many
types of service, such as becoming a fraternity house-
mother and organizing a nursing home.

In an effort to help mother, I invited her to ac-
company me to some conferences where a spiritual
climate might hopefully give her a sense of direction.
Over a period of several years, we attended eight or
nine meetings, with mother loving the people but unable to buy any of the religious jargon.

Then we went to a meeting where Tommy Tyson,
a Methodist evangelist, was the speaker. One evening
he spoke with simplicity and great power about Jesus

and our need to be willing to follow him at all costs. "If you are willing to die to the world, to give up all material possessions, comfort, family, friends, security; if you love Jesus and can trust your life completely to him, come, and lay your life down on the altar."

"Let's go," mother whispered to me. Knowing her and her past reactions to evangelists and altar calls, I thought she meant *let's go out*. I said: "You go, if you want to, but I want to stay here."

Mother stood up, made her way around and over my knees to the aisle, but instead of turning left, turned right and down to the front of the church. To my grateful surprise, I watched my proper sixty-seven-year-old mother stand before the altar in childlike faith and commit all that she knew of herself to all that she knew of Almighty God.

Some time later I received this letter from her:

Dear Ruth,

I didn't write this letter earlier telling of my plans because I didn't want to be stopped. After making my commitment, I went home and wondered how. I asked myself the question, how do I give up my bed, my home, my friends, my security, my family—and for what? Today watching TV, I had the answer.

I have joined the Peace Corps. I will be going to serve in India for two years.

Love,
Mother

Nothing did stop her. At the age of sixty-seven, she went as a Peace Corps volunteer to India.

Shortly after she arrived there, it was discovered that she was a registered nurse. She was immediately placed in the hospital (which turned out to be little more than a large open warehouse-type building with a minimum of sanitation and medication).

During her two years in India, mother became a servant of the impoverished sick. With a stubborn determination to improve the situation, she begged, borrowed, and traded for materials, for time from local workers, and for bureaucratic permission to make necessary changes. After two years, it was time for her to leave India. But in that short period more than thirty of her projects were completed. The hospital now had partitions for separate quarters—the doctors' offices, the outpatient clinic, the surgery, the reception room and the examining room.

Mother was surprised when she again put feet down on American soil. She had supposed, when she departed, that she was abandoning her world of abundance. But she came back a richer person with a greater sense of the goodness of life. Her act of "giving all" resulted in her having more. She had discovered in her sacrifice the truth of Jesus' promise, "He who loses his life for my sake will find it."[1] Christ means what he says.

After her return to the United States, mother was invited to lecture around the country. She told of her work with its frustration and satisfaction. She introduced many to the beautiful people of India, calling for harmony between the people of India and the United States. Mother's new life began at an age when many people have lost their sense of purpose in life.

Obviously, God doesn't think in terms of chronological age. Life begins with death to one's selfish desires. When mother's purpose became set by her commitment to serve, her service was under divine orders. Her restlessness and lack of inner joy disappeared. The miracle is easy to reconstruct: the moment she saw beyond her problem to the possibility of abandoning her will to God's will, she began to experience an expansion of her vistas. She saw life differently; she defined it differently. There was still brokenness, darkness and death in the world. But now she saw that, by the grace of God, her job and joy was to do something about it. That vision always brings immeasurable blessing to life.

LEARNING TO SEE CHRIST IN EVERYTHING

Our highest purpose is to do God's will. There is no need to know in some mystical way at every turn what that will is. All that is needed is the will to do that will. Rarely does anyone perceive God's will clearly in the moment. But the most uncertain can desire that will. And in that desire lies the certainty of guidance. It is always given. It may be hidden from the rational mind but it is always there. "I will instruct you and teach you in the way which you should go, I will counsel you with my eye upon you"[2] is a promise we can depend on, and we must depend on it to experience the joy which eludes the drifting and aimless.

There is a sense, however, in which we do know exactly what God's will is. It is to seek Christ in every face, every relationship, every experience, and never despair of finding him—this is our ultimate joy. It is the brightest thread in the fabric of life.

Jesus told us this in parables, in sermons, in every action of his life. "Seek first his [God's] kingdom," "Love one another as I have loved you," "Love the Lord your God with all your heart, . . . soul, . . .

strength, and . . . mind."[3] Old Testament prophets had called men to this high way. Jesus gave that revelation flesh and blood.

Five hundred years before our Lord came to earth in physical form, Buddha directed his followers to "see God in everything—and everything in God." But that leaves the mind grasping for a concrete definition of God! Jesus solved that problem for us. He is the Christ, the definition of God our minds can embrace. So, we seek to see Christ in everything—and everything in Christ. The kind of love he lived is "poured into our hearts through the Holy Spirit,"[4] so that we can live that love where it makes a practical difference: in our kitchen, in the office, in our bedroom, with our children, with our aging parents, even in hateful community crises.

If such Christlike purpose eludes you, remember: purpose arises from the direction of the will, and will involves a mind-set. It is possible for you to set your mind on Christ while you read these words. You can begin to practice the presence of Christ in every contact you make. Will to share and see Christ in the electrician, the grocery store clerk, your child's teacher, the garage mechanic, the druggist, the garbage collector, in everybody. Watch the differences in their reactions when you speak to them as if they were Christ. You can set your mind to honor the Christ-in-them which faith sees.[5]

You will also see a subtle change in your own reactions to others; you elevate your attitude when you accept this high purpose. It won't be consistent. You will often slip into the old pattern of reacting to people on their merit or worth to you. But keep on. Your purpose firmly held will win out, and the capacity to see Christ in the gross and unattractive will grow.

William James has said, "What holds attention governs action." If Christ can hold your attention, he can govern your action. And that attention is usually an act of the will. Will involves choice. Who will be your model, your ideal, your reference point for your life? Is it Jesus Christ? Then if you keep calling your thoughts back to him, you will discover your attention span toward him growing, and your purpose and quality of life deepening. You will find that he acts toward you like a loving shepherd who moves all his sheep to the right pasture, the still water, the safe fold.

THE PURPOSE OF BECOMING WHOLE

Christ's goal for us is wholeness. So all we need to do is agree with God that we need and want to be whole. But the reason we don't experience life in its fullness is that we don't make wholeness our goal. That takes commitment to the master builder. It demands that we say to Christ, "Not my plans but yours be followed."

There is a blueprint for wholeness for each of us. Though it may seem rather vague to us, it is clear to Christ. He sees each unique quality in us and knows each piece of material which must go into our lives. If we try to define our lives by comparing them to the spiritual growth of others, we're using a wrong blueprint. Many lives have become monstrously misshapen because they tried to make themselves into a cookie-cutter version of someone else. We are not a copy of anyone else. We have our own individual greatness which will emerge only as we cooperate with our maker and builder.

In his essay on *Self Reliance*, Emerson commented,

"There is at this moment for you an utterance brave and grand as that of the colossal chisel of Phidias, or trowel of the Egyptians [the pyramids] or the pen of Moses or Dante, but different from all these." We must learn to rest, not in comparisons, contrasts, or defective yardsticks, but in the confidence that "no eye has seen, nor ear heard . . . what God has prepared for those who love him."[6] His individual attention to each detail of our lives is emphasized in the commands to "be anxious for nothing," and "in everything give thanks," acknowledging his control over our lives.[7] Then as surely as the lilies are clothed and the falling sparrow noted, just as surely will we be loved and provided for as the divine plan for our life emerges.

Never forget that to will God's will places us in his care and under his direction. By willing to do his will, we entrust the responsibility of the outcome of our experiences to him.

My mother at age sixty-seven found new wholeness by dedicating herself to a high purpose. Christ healed her from within as her will was committed to do his will. New life begins for all of us at this place, whatever our age or condition.

FINDING NEW PURPOSE IN ADOLESCENCE

My twenty-year-old son had a different experience. He had already willed to follow Christ but he needed emotional release through inner healing.

During Scotty's high school years he constantly seemed to flounder without a clear sense of purpose. His total life was immersed in athletics, but beneath the glory of the superlatives used to describe his basketball prowess, he came to see the emptiness, the temporariness of it all. His struggle to find his identity and his purpose, however, was very slow in coming.

Two days before my daughter's wedding, Scotty, then a junior at Syracuse University, flew home. On his first night home, he said, "Mother, I have a lot of things on my mind, and I want to reserve some time with you tomorrow morning at eight o'clock." I swallowed hard—as if I had nothing planned and nothing to do on the day before my daughter's wedding! But I knew his need was great, so I accepted the appointment.

"But, Mother," he added, "I don't want to talk at home. We'll be disturbed here. I need to be completely alone with you."

So the next morning we went across town to the only place we could find where we could talk without interruption—a motel room.

As soon as we had settled in, he said, "Mother, I want to tell you what has been happening in my life, my problems, my pains, my scars, and some healings that have been taking place."

From eight o'clock in the morning until five o'clock that afternoon, he told me of his strengths and of his weaknesses. He elaborated on his habit patterns before college, his overcompensating, his abilities to manipulate and use people. After he went to college, he decided to find out for the first time if anyone would like him for himself. His rebellion toward college, the establishment, the injustices of the world poured out. He shared with me the different ways he had lashed out at the world because he didn't know how to cope with it. When he confessed that on several occasions he had stood on the twentieth floor of his dormitory wanting to jump, I could feel the hair rise on the back of my neck and my heart start to pound.

Around noon Scotty said, "I guess you'd like to know where I am *right now*. Mother, I have a vision of what I'm going to become."

"Yes?" I didn't dare say more.

"I can only share the vision because I'm not there yet, but I'm on the right path." His psychological understanding of himself amazed me. Even the trials he had experienced with me, and those I had with him, were incorporated into his plan of growth and healing. I was suddenly grateful for the number of hours I had spent in prayer for him. My son was becoming a man, a man with a Christlike vision for his life.

At five o'clock we returned home. To my relief and delight, the wedding preparations hadn't collapsed in my absence.

Two months later, when he returned home from college for the summer, I asked Scotty if he would allow me to guide him with Jesus through the years when his pain was so great. I knew he still needed to have Jesus heal the open wounds of the past. I told him he needed to stand with Jesus at the open window of the twentieth story of the dormitory, to remove his fears, to ease and then to remove all sense of failure, all frustration, the memory of all the years of manipulating others and his consequent feelings of self-hatred. Through his creative imagination he had to let the Spirit demolish the ugly mental structures he had erected and reconstruct a new self-image.

Yes, he replied, he wanted such healing. With a mother's love and faith, I prayed. And after we had finished, I knew that his inner life had been touched. Although we've never discussed those hours, I see my son today as a maturing, vibrant, young man equipped to experience any upheaval or frustration in life. He knows from experience that there is a purpose in everything, and that this purpose gives him the discipline to find his ultimate goal.

PURPOSE BEYOND FAILURE

Frustration and failure are feelings that bully the heart. We can easily become brutalized by them into believing a lie. We can begin to feel that we are just losers. But the truth is that in Christ we cannot fail. St. Paul is right, "We are more than conquerors through him who loved us"[8]—more than winners. Failure is a mirage. The heat in the desert of our spirits makes the mirage of failure appear, but it will vanish if we take the time to advance toward it with our eyes open. It will prove really to be a door to success. And there are no permanently locked doors of blessing in the kingdom of God—only unused keys. Closed doors help us to look for those keys. The key may be greater faith, love, service to others, honesty, fellowship, prayers, meditation, or inner healing. But the question to ask when a door is temporarily locked is not, "Why have I failed?" That is needless nonsense. The question should be, "Where is the key to open the door?" That is faith, which always leads to great blessing.

At one point in my life I had an overwhelming desire to be a schoolteacher. My four children were growing up and I had time on my hands. I enrolled in college to complete the requirements for a Bachelor of Arts degree. I struggled through Algebra III and two years of French with tears and prayer, and through trigonometry with even more tears and desperate prayer. After years away from the classroom, I found studying an agonizing discipline. But at last I earned both a degree and a teaching certificate in secondary education.

But my troubles, I discovered, graduated along with me. I was hired to teach tenth and eleventh grade English, and when I walked before my students, I felt as though I were standing before a firing squad. My greatest fear had always come from standing before a group of people. And just standing in front of these students panicked me. But beyond the trembling knees and dry mouth I was a determined young woman. I wanted to teach, and I had the high purpose of introducing these youth, somehow, to the master teacher. The paralyzing fear fled. I began to teach.

It was a hard year for me. I didn't know how expert I was as a teacher but *I* was learning a lot. My relationship with the students was good. I began to settle down inside, secure in the knowledge that I was now well on my way to success in my chosen profession.

When my contract came up for renewal at the end of my first year, my principal called me into his office. After a somewhat uncomfortable pause, he said, "Ruth, before I renew your contract, I must ask you one question, 'Do you intend to *teach* or *preach?*' "

My moment of glory came as I looked him in the eye, straightened up to my full height of five feet two inches, and replied, "I intend to preach."

That was not a professionally safe answer. But it was honest. The principal seemed very relieved. "That makes it considerably easier for me because the head of the English department has reported: 'Ruth is the greatest failure I've had in my English department in twenty-six years.' "

I was unprepared for that blow. I turned toward

the door and walked out. During the drive of five blocks from the school to my husband's office, I couldn't keep the tears back. After my husband quieted me somewhat and tried to console me, I announced to him that my life was over. Who can live with the thought of being "the greatest failure in twenty-six years," in one's chosen field? My only alternative was to preach—and I had no place to preach.

For two weeks I bathed my ego in self-pitying tears. Then I came to myself. I began to realize that I was pounding on a door when all I needed was a key. My life was in God's hands. He called me to this life and to his purposes before I entered into my mother's womb. With this awareness I began to affirm, "Jesus, I trust you." That was the key.

Two weeks after my dismissal I was asked to teach a Bible class at Ft. Bragg, the military base in my hometown of Fayetteville, North Carolina. Then I was invited to teach another. Finally I was teaching five such groups. I had been called to be a teacher all right. I simply had to learn what kind.

That was just the important beginning. Soon I received invitations to participate in several small retreats. This led to requests to lead retreats. Now, because I was a "failure," I am called to minister in every part of the world. "Trust and obey" says the old hymn. That is our only need when facing failure.

The truth that proved to be the key to the door away from a teaching career was that God knew me before I was ever conceived.[9] This truth allows me to give thanks for my birth, my parents, my background and for every experience of life and each significant person as a part of that life. Each of us must trust God's vision to see what we cannot see. We must accept the guidance of the God who has known us always and promises to lead and perfect his children.

THE NECESSITY OF PURPOSE

Dr. Viktor Frankl discovered in the midst of the torture and inhumanities of a Nazi concentration camp that one of the deepest motivations of the human personality is to discover a meaning for living. Among the prisoners he found that only those who had a purpose beyond themselves could maintain both their life and their humanity. It shocked him when he observed that many of his fellow prisoners were dying of no clinically definable disease. They had simply lost the will to live.

This same characteristic was noted by Dorothy Thompson, the noted Roman Catholic, in her study of the life of concentration camp prisoners immediately after World War II. To her shock she found that many prisoners had collaborated with their Nazi tormentors in the torture and liquidation of fellow prisoners. Upon the promise of a few days, or few weeks, more of life, many prisoners were willing to sell their humanity, to become inhuman persecutors. Doctors, educators, blue collar workers, people from almost every kind of background cooperated in the inhuman torture and murder of fellow prisoners—except for one group. This group had an almost perfect record for unwillingness to harm anyone. They were the priests and ministers of the gospel. Thompson's conclusion was the same as Dr. Frankl's—that the transcendent purpose of their lives to serve Christ and their fellow man was the difference between their humanity and the inhumanity of the other prisoners.

We all desire to understand life, to discover its

meaning. Years pass in the blur of activities. Seldom do we take time to view our life as a great design longing to unfold, a great plan made by the master planner. But this is the truth, and life is a tenuous experience without such a perspective. Most of us have been spared the horrors of a concentration camp. But the soul is imprisoned until it is liberated by decisive spiritual purpose.

I remember my first fumbling attempts to find new purpose for my life. I had gone to church all my life, was married, with four children. If you had asked me what my greatest need was at this time, I would have told you that I was unhappy without knowing why, that I had no reason to be unhappy. I would have said that my one great need was to get away from home, from problems, from all the everyday menial tasks. But I would not have been precise about my needs and wants. The good news, though, is that dissatisfaction can lead to definition of purpose, if the dissatisfaction leads to a quest for truth and not escape.

Now I had to determine two things: which direction I would take in this search, and what was the ultimate goal I desired.

I have come to know in these past two years that God's timing is perfect, that he watches over us even when we are unaware of his providence, and that he answers our requests before we ask. But as I indicated, at this point, I only knew that I needed to get away from everyone and everything that to me was a part of my problem.

A friend in a newly formed prayer group I had discovered told me that a retreat was being held on the North Carolina coast. Because I was a church member, I thought I would feel at home here, would get some rest, meet different people, and get my thoughts together without the domestic pressures I was feeling.

The retreat lasted for a week. The people were from many different denominations. Having been raised all my life in the narrow experience of one denomination I found this a strange experience.

I was surprised to find at this retreat that every day began with praise and joy and ended on the same high note. The program was subject to change as the mood of the camp changed. (Songs, speeches, conversation at mealtime.) All moved in harmony with the growing experience of the participants. More surprising, these people acted as though they knew Jesus Christ personally. They loved one another and shared intimately from their own negative and positive personal experiences.

I remember on Sunday morning the uneasiness I felt when I went down to the service in casual sportswear. But I found that everyone else was dressed casually. That may seem insignificant to many. But not to me; I was rigidly conditioned to equate worship with formality—no small breakthrough. Never had I known a group to be so full of love and so open to one another. None seemed a stranger to the others. And although I was new to the group, I was no stranger. They shared their joy, their love, and their problems as a family. I found it difficult to believe what I was seeing and feeling.

It was in one of the prayer groups which met each afternoon that the emotional shell I had built around me began to break. In this particular prayer meeting, we were asked to believe and pray for the expressed need of each individual in turn, but focusing attention on Jesus Christ. There was something very real about this exercise, yet when it came my turn to tell these people my needs, cold fear took over. My inner world was falling apart, and how desperately I wanted to reach out. But I couldn't. All eyes were on me and I didn't know what to say. When finally I was able to speak, all I could remember was a point in the morning talk. The speaker had taught us about the fruits of the Spirit.

Evasively, I said, "Please pray for me, that I might receive the fruit of the Spirit." The leader looked a bit quizzical and asked, "Which fruit do you want?" I had to admit I didn't know. She had not intended to embarrass me. So, she began to name them as they are listed in Galatians: "love, joy, peace, patience, kindness, goodness, faithfulness, gentleness, self-control."[10]

Love. I had never known how to love, not really. *Joy.* I had felt so little joy. *Peace.* How I craved this elusive experience.

As the leader completed the catalog of these spiritual fruits, I was overcome with emotion.

"I want all of them," I said, and I meant it.

"Well," she responded, "we ought never to limit God. We'll pray that you receive all of them."

She invited me to sit in a chair in the center of the circle. These new and different friends gathered around me. Some placed their hands on my head and shoulders. All stood in silent intercession as one led aloud in prayer.

What the leader knew, and I did not, was that I was inviting Jesus Christ to enter my life. And that is precisely what happened. I gave my life to Christ. (I recall a similar moment of commitment when I was a little girl of ten.)

As that prayer group offered its prayer for me, the first I had ever received, I was saying a new and decisive *yes* to that earlier spiritual birth. I was allowing the Savior of my childhood to become the Lord of my adult life. In that new relationship with Christ I found the missing purpose for my life.

After leaving the camp, I reflected upon what had happened. I knew that those people I had met were different. My observation of them had created a fresh sense of need. My purpose arose out of this need. I didn't have the love they knew, didn't know their joy. I wasn't like they were. I had seen Jesus in them. Jesus Christ had not lived in me nor controlled me. And I knew this was what I was searching for. I knew that I would never stop searching until I could know this reality. Even though I could not have expressed it then, or defined it, I had found new purpose: to be a servant of Christ and others.

9.

The Healing Power of
SERVING

The role of the servant is held in rather low esteem in our society. One doesn't expect to find the name of a domestic in *Who's Who*. But Jesus considered himself a servant to every person. And ever since, loving servitude has been the ultimate measure of greatness.

Jesus' definition of *servant* shows it to be more an attitude than a profession. The servant chooses to set aside his or her own needs and wants to attend to the needs of others.

Jesus was practical. He rarely called people to the asceticism of such religious leaders as John the Baptist. He said he came to give men a superabundant life.[1] Consequently we consider the healing power of serving in this context. Servanthood, appraised in advance, can appear to be debasing. In this sense it can teach us humility. Servanthood, appraised in action, is a direct, clearcut means to a great, creative, rich, whole life.

THE IDEAL MODEL FOR SERVICE

Many people are given inadequate models of selfless service from their infancy. The baby, living in a self-centered world, needs food, diapers changed, body cleaned, and a lot of tender loving care. It is unable to give. Maturity is in great measure a state of consciousness where selfless giving rather than infantile selfish getting governs one's life.

One mark of emotional illness in an adult is regression to the infant incapacity to give beyond that world walled in by self. Total incapacity is psychotic. For example, when Dr. E. Stanley Jones asked the patients of a mental hospital to roll bandages for the troops overseas during World War II, not one person volunteered. Mental health and the capacity to serve are directly related.

When mother and daddy are emotionally mature, they enjoy giving to the baby, and to the child as it develops. But if parents are neurotic, the child will hear or sense a lot of "Don't bother me," "I haven't got time," "I'm busy," "That's mine, you can't have it," "Why do you always have to come in just when I'm watching my favorite program?"

The whole sad litany of selfishness which infects so many homes imprints on a child's consciousness the idea that life is an experience of grabbing the best because "you only live once," and of letting others take what is left. There is no inner healing without erasing that kind of pattern from the subconscious and reconditioning it to see service as one of the highest, most fulfilling roles in life.

Jesus is the perfect model of such emotional wholeness.

HEALING ATTITUDES TOWARD SERVICE

After I committed my life to serve Christ, I had a dream of what that life of service would be. No longer would I spend my time in what then seemed to me the meaningless, "unspiritual" activities of clubs, gardening, meetings, and parties. Now I would be about the important business of life. I would visit hospitals, pray for the sick, teach and preach. How little I understood God's definition of service.

His path to greater enlightenment began when my Baptist church called me to work in the nursery. Suddenly my great service to God was reduced to serving crying babies with dirty diapers. But that is where I had to begin.

Many of my adult years had already been spent serving in the church nursery, since it was the responsibility of young mothers to undertake this task. And I hated the job. But I had said, "Lord, I'll go wherever you say, and I'll do whatever you instruct." Now I wanted to say, "But Lord, I didn't mean working in the nursery."

Every Sunday for that year I resented going to the nursery. At the end of the year, I felt sure that I had not only served Christ, but had served my time. I had done my duty out of a sense of responsibility. Now I wanted to do something I felt to be important.

The shocker came when I was asked to work a second year in the nursery. Another year? I didn't want to stay there another week. But by now, I knew that even a diaper derby could be sanctified and that there was something I had to learn there. I had to face situations that I needed for the healing of negative attitudes I had failed to come to grips with during my first year.

Jesus instructed us to "love one another." This must certainly mean that he wants each of us to serve out of love. It gradually dawned on me that because this job was the one thing I hated most to do, the nursery was exactly the right place for me. I needed a lot of my attitudes changed. And God was beginning with mine toward such menial service.

So I set about to change. I went to the nursery early on Sunday morning. I identified each baby by name and determined that I would love and serve each child. It was a gradual process. I soon began to see each baby as a human being rather than an undersized, overwhelming problem wrapped in a blanket. I began to enjoy each Sunday and to look forward to seeing my little wards. By the end of the year I was not only willing but excited about moving into a third year of that responsibility.

Then I had a call from a church official: "Ruth, we'd like to change your job for the new year. Would you work in the kitchen on Wednesday night suppers? The hostess has resigned." Since Peg Bracken's *I Hate to Cook Book* was my favorite domestic text, you can see that this was another area in which I needed an attitude change.

The job, which I accepted, required that I plan the meals, buy the groceries, prepare the food, and serve the meal for two hundred people each Wednesday night. At that time, I was finding it a difficult challenge to prepare and serve a meal for my family of six. How could I enjoy serving let alone loving the job of ministerial mess sergeant for that crowd? But God and I did it, and I grew to enjoy it. It turned out to be a happy learning experience.

Brother Lawrence tells how he learned to wash pots and pans to the glory of God. From his book *Practicing the Presence of God* I learned that I, a person who could not get a meal on the table for six people, could ask, "Jesus, how many bottles of catsup does it take to make meat loaf for two hundred people?" It always turned out right if not gourmet glorious. I learned that if I trusted him in every detail of planning and preparing the meals, he was just as much in that experience as I have seen him in making the blind see and the deaf hear. The secret is to accept Christ's exalted view of servitude when a job is humanly insignificant.

THE CALL TO SERVE

Christ's call to service is clear. But too often we object. If we are called to go out and speak for him, we make the same response as Moses did, "O Lord, I can't speak." Moses had a pretty valid excuse—he stuttered.

But excuses don't count. A national conference speaker used to stutter so badly it was almost impossible to understand what he was saying. But when God called him to this profession, he chose not to let stuttering keep him from public speaking. When he went into the pulpit, he gave his best. This man was the one God used to reach my rebellious heart, because through his stammering words I heard the Spirit of Christ's love irresistably proclaimed.

It is not oratorical eloquence God needs. It is the person who will speak out of obedience and love. The gifted often find it more difficult to depend on God's Spirit. And submission to the mastery of Christ is what makes the messenger of Christ effective.

People ask, "Ruth, don't you get frightened before you speak?" Frightened! I felt such fear at my first large conference that I fainted shortly before I went on to the platform. And even now I find myself bombarding heaven with prayer before I speak: "Lord, I'm willing to speak for you. Lord, I'm willing to fail. Lord, I'm willing to be a fool for your sake. Lord, I'm willing . . ." Apparently I'm in good company, because Helen Hayes says she always gets butterflies in her stomach before going on stage but has learned to put them in formation! I sometimes get screaming eagles in my stomach. But Christ always tames them when I turn them over to him.

SERVING FROM WEAKNESS

When I was teaching one of my first Bible classes out at Ft. Bragg, I tried hard to be sensitive to the problems and needs of the girls who came every Thursday, to give them adequate answers and encouragement and inspiration. They looked upon me as a person of spiritual and emotional strength. Quite often they came by my house for prayer and counseling.

One particular day, I was in a low period emotionally, trying to work out a problem. I had been in tears for a couple of hours, when I heard a knock at the door. Drying my eyes and trying to clear my emotions, I opened the door to find Vera, one of the class leaders. She was a great help in the Bible class, and I had worked with her growth and development for quite some time.

I apologized profusely for having been caught a

little bit under the weather emotionally. Vera tried to make me comfortable by saying she just wanted to have a cup of coffee—she really didn't have a big problem that day. So, we sat and talked and shared for an hour or two. We were both laughing and happy and light by the time she left.

As I took Vera to the door, I apologized again. "I hope the next time you come I won't be having a problem myself, and I'll be able to help you more."

Vera called me after she got home and had had time to think over the afternoon. "Ruth, as many times as I have been to you for counseling, and as many times as I have asked for help, and all the times you've prayed for me, I don't think that you've ever been as much help to me as you were this afternoon. Because you allowed me to see you in your weakness at a very low point, in a way, something fell in place with my own life. I knew there would be times when I would feel down, but I never thought that *you* ever had any moments of weakness. I thought you always were on top of every situation. So, I really thank you more for today than for any of the time we've ever spent together."

Many of us may fear the idea of service because we feel unworthy, inexperienced, ignorant, or untrained. None of these reasons is valid. Who of us is strong enough to serve people as Christ did? We are all weak and inadequate. But God has the wonderful ability to use our weaknesses to help the weak. After our pains and weaknesses have been overcome, we can help others who have been similarly afflicted, without pity or condescension and with understanding. When we are dependent upon God, he can even use us in the midst of our suffering to help others afflicted with similar pain.

Drug addicts and other emotional cripples who have been touched by Christ's love are the ablest in helping others in their tragic subculture. This is the principle behind Jesus' charge to Simon Peter. In effect, he said, "You're going to deny me but when you are restored and turned to me again, I want you to strengthen and build up your brothers."[2]

Weakness overcome makes us stronger, but it also makes us more acceptable to one similarly suffering. This does not mean that the person who has never been crippled in a particular area is less a candidate for service. The more fortunate can be made more compassionate. Servanthood helps them grow in the knowledge that their goodness contrasted to Christ's makes them appear to be no better than the prodigal. Lukewarm love lies at the heart of most of the world's unmoved mountains—grief, ghettos, poverty, disease, war. Serving helps us identify with the more obviously unfortunate. Then we will learn from the Spirit how to reach down to help serve the fallen without ever appearing to stoop. Serving fosters humility which knows we are no better than the broken. To combine this with love which wills that men be whole is the credential for effective, redemptive, healing service.

When we have this spirit of humility and love, we do not need to go out looking for those in need. We will be drawn to them. When we sense God saying to us, as he did to Isaiah, "Whom shall I send to the needy; who will go for me?" we will respond, "Here am I, send me."[3] Events and circumstances will unfold that will reveal limitless opportunities for service. The truth is that many are called but few stand up to be chosen for service. When we do, the Lord of the harvest will keep us busy but not burdened.

At one of her healing services, not long before she died, Katherine Kuhlman was praying for a large group of ministers who had been invited up on the stage. As she stepped up to place her hands on one minister, he drew back. "You're not going to pray for me," he protested.

"Why, not?" she asked.

"Because you're a woman preacher and I don't believe in them."

"I don't either," Miss Kuhlman said. "I truly believe," she continued, "that years ago, God tapped a man on the shoulder and asked him, 'Will you go throughout the land and tell the people of my power to heal?' And he refused. So, he went to another man and then another and another until finally he ran out of men. Then he asked me and I said yes."

Whether or not the scenario is absolutely as she described it, her understanding of God's purpose to use the willing, regardless of sex, is true. Her life was singularly used because she made herself totally available to Jesus Christ as a servant to the sick. He is ready to use us just as fully.

PERSONAL REWARDS FROM SERVICE

As we reach out to help another, inner healing can be triggered or accelerated. Willingness to serve is one of the many lessons our Lord was teaching us through the emblem of broken bread and poured out wine. When we say, "Lord, use me," we are saying, "Lord, break me, make me usable." As soon as we are willing to be broken for others, our own emotional needs are met more rapidly and richly. And repressed needs often surface under the stimulus of selfless service.

For a long time I could only faintly remember the

first nine years of my life. I had deeply repressed most of that period until one day a man came to me for prayer for inner healing. As we sat there face to face, I took his hands and prayed, "Jesus, we place this time together in your care and ask that you reveal the deep, painful memories that are blocked. Help him that he may be free to express them. We claim the healing . . . Amen."

As he began to share his life with me, I realized that his narrative was uncovering forgotten memories from my early childhood. Moments of pain surfaced for me to see, which in turn eliminated some of the dark mental patterns that were out of harmony with Christ's Spirit. Until that revelation, I had felt helpless to understand or change them. As the prayer of St. Francis says, "It is in giving that we receive." That is how I received that day for that need.

Just as there is fulfillment in serving others which nothing else can bring, so there is a beauty in people hidden from the unconcerned or the merely curious. Only the caring can enter the rich inner soul sanctum of another. When one comes with the quiet listening spirit committed to unconditional love, the image of God appears in another, even through the shadows of an imperfect heart. The cynic sees only the imperfections, and therefore sees humanity as deserving of destruction. Jesus sees through the imperfections to the image of God, and so he loved all of us enough to die so we might live. We see less clearly than he. But when we give our lives to others we catch glimpses, we have visionary moments, when plain and broken people reveal their beauty and make our lives more beautiful.

Robert Browning illuminates this spiritual truth in his poem "My Star":

All that I know
　Of a certain star
Is, it can throw
　(Like the angled spar)
Now a dart of red,
　Now a dart of blue
Till my friends have said
　They would fain see, too,
My star which dartles the red and blue!
Then it stops like a bird; like a flower, hangs furled.
　They must solace themselves with the Saturn above
　　it.
What matter to me if their star is a world?
　Mine has opened its soul to me; therefore I love it.

SERVING THE LONELY

Unfortunately, a great many of us do not experience the sharing of two lives through caring that Browning describes. We experience only loneliness. The heart can feel such pain from experiences of rejection in childhood that we form the illusion that nobody cares, nobody understands, nobody can be trusted. Consequently there is a battle between our fear of being hurt and our need to be accepted and loved. A person in this state requires the faithful, careful overtures of someone who cares. Often the lonely, rejection-conditioned person will reach out and then withdraw, or will reach out and then lash out. Anger, guilt, and fear conspire to destroy the thing the lonely person wants most—a loving relationship. Serving the lonely demands sensitivity to hear the cry for help behind the cool or hostile demeanor and to get past the barrier of such a person.

Althea was wrestling with brutal feelings of loneliness. Overwhelmed by her struggle and having no one to turn to, she cried out, "Jesus, you know I am so alone and I need somebody so much. Please help me!"

She sat in her empty house waiting, listening for someone to come. Nothing happened. No one came. In the agonizing emptiness and silence, the image of a person kept reappearing in her mind. She was not sure what was driving her to contact this person. But she finally picked up the phone and called her.

"Are you busy?" Althea asked the friend.

"Yes, I have dinner guests," was the answer, "but I'm not too busy to talk."

Retreating, Althea said, "Oh, it's nothing. It wasn't important. I'll talk to you later."

Althea hung up the phone and sat staring at the wall still wondering why she had made the fruitless call. A short time later the back door opened. In walked her friend, took her hand, walked her out onto the back porch, sat down, and took her into her arms. For three hours Althea cried in her friend's arms. To someone sensitive enough not to be fooled by her precipitous withdrawal over the phone, Althea confessed through her tears the bitterness, the resentments, the hates she felt for all those who had been cruel to her. All of the years of loneliness came out.

"She just held me," Althea told me later, "and let me cry. She let me scream and get it all out, and when I was through, I felt someone cared. I wasn't alone any more. I felt Jesus had heard my prayer and that he was really with me, too."

No one can measure how much that moment of caring and service did for Althea. It was a priceless gift to her. Such listening and just "being" is crucial. Since "God is love," and Love is God, as we extend a helping heart, we enable God to be present to others through our humanity.

SUGGESTIONS FOR SERVING THE LONELY

Dr. Eric Fromm, the noted psychiatrist, has said that the greatest repression in our society is not sex but loneliness. Because loneliness is so widespread, it is important that we know how to be a servant to the lonely.

(1) The most important word is *listen*. Don't probe. Don't try to solve their problem or analyze their actions. The lonely are extremely sensitive to rejection. And any effort on our part, however benevolent, to change or correct them could be construed as rejection.

(2) When angers surface, when accusations are made against significant people in their lives, let them ventilate. But don't get caught up in their angers. Pray for understanding. Often the offended unconsciously have sought out the negativity about which they complain. But before they can gain insights into their anger, they must receive unconditional love in large doses. This does not mean supporting their antagonisms. It does mean continually assuring them that though you don't have the answers, you care and God cares, and that answers will be given in time.

(3) If the person is open to prayer, pray with them, asking the Holy Spirit to bring the presence of Jesus Christ into their life to banish their loneliness. Then encourage them to offer a prayer of forgiveness for those who have rejected and offended them. If they don't feel up to this, and usually they don't, assure them that simply being willing to forgive, without feeling forgiveness, is an effective first step to for-

giveness and personal inner healing. If they are unwilling even to will to forgive, they are not ready to find release from their loneliness. Predictably, they will withdraw into their self-imposed emotional exile for a time. But your prayers can continue to embrace them until they make the first step toward forgiveness. Only as they are willing to forgive can they begin to make a break with the past memories which create their present loneliness.

When the person responds positively to the prayer and to the act of forgiving, it is well for you to conclude you sharing with a single sentence of affirmative prayer: "Thank you, Lord Jesus Christ, for healing (name of person)." Jesus promised us "that if two of you on earth agree about anything you ask for, it will be done for you by my Father in heaven."⁴ Seal the experience of catharsis and inner reconstruction with that agreement.

However, even when one knows the areas in another which need healing, it is not possible to be sure in advance how to pray, or what specifically needs prayer. Each prayer must be an experience of spiritual guidance. There is no absolute technique. So, perhaps the most important prayer we can offer by way of preparation is for the spiritual knowledge and discernment which allows the precision needed to catalyze inner healing—ours or someone else's who may need our helping hand. As we move along, willing to serve in Christ's name, we will be able to trust the Spirit to teach us all we need in order to bring about wholeness. We also can trust the Spirit to delay healing until the proper season. Jesus spoke with tender eloquence about how his Father opulently clothed the lilies of the field. He was challenging us to trust God to care for our needs more richly.⁵ Similarly he will remove the tattered rags of our impoverished emotions and clothe our minds with love, joy and peace.

SERVICE THROUGH THE BODY OF CHRIST

Perhaps no atmosphere is more conducive to creative service than that of a small group where there is an element of personal commitment to the welfare of the other members. And when we add the dimension of Christ's Spirit, we find the ultimate source of service. This spiritual service group is what the New Testament calls the Body of Christ. St. Paul said that we find our significance in this Body by how we serve the whole. Just as the more humble parts of the physical body receive honor as an essential part of the whole physical function, all are glorified by service in the Body of Christ. Service, no matter how humble, deserves honor and respect.[6]

Silent Service

Among the most therapeutic disciplines we can undertake is to try everyday to do something for someone else, without telling anyone what we have done. This "magnificent obsession" is more easily achieved as a part of a group discipline. In fact, in any new discipline, from calorie counting to meditation, we will find advantages in being reinforced by like-purposed people.

In the spiritual setting there is what someone has called "synergy," a collective energy which is unmistakably more potent than the power of the sum of all individuals in the group. This synergy not only operates in the gathered group experience, but it can also be felt in the group-related activities undertaken by individuals away from the other members. The obvious prohibition against verbally sharing our deeds of service with the other members does not diminish the power of this group exercise; it increases it.

Listening to Silence

Another kind of hidden, humble ministry deserves honor which is rarely given it. That is, listening to another person's silence. Much is said by the needy spirit which cannot be expressed verbally or which can be obscured by a clutter of words. The ability to do this is a gift.

Speaking to a large audience, a lecturer noticed a young man he had never met seated toward the front of the auditorium. Sitting down at the conclusion of his talk, he found his attention riveted on him. He began to sense the pain of the stranger's heart.

At the meeting's end, people came up to thank the speaker. One of them was the young man. As he shook his hand, the speaker heard himself saying, "Do you know how much your father loves you? Do you know how much he needs you?" The young man broke down on the spot. Only the day before, after a bitter argument, he had spurned his father's efforts to be reconciled to him. He knew that God had shown the speaker that he was blind to his father's love.

GOAL OF INNER HEALING

We have said that one of the rewards of service is our own healing. But it is possible to let our own desire to be healed become the center of our attention. If that happens, we need to find a new focus. Healing should not be sought as an end in itself.

"Whosoever seeks to save his life," said Jesus, "will lose it."[7] Healing is life-saving, but by itself it causes a self-centeredness which can be deadly. Jesus must remain our first love, our focus. Healing is the by-product of this perspective. If we turn our full attention to desiring God's will, out of our obedience we can expect to find peace and joy.

The chief reason service is a superior path to healing is that it makes healing a by-product rather than the goal. Disease (dis-ease) of body or mind is a divine attention-getter. All of our painful symptoms are calling us back to our Source. At very least, they make us see our need for God. Even a doctor can become divine surrogate if we have a heart that can sense the truth. But if healing comes as we reach out to help another, we have a running head start on our goal of always seeking the will of God, the kingdom of God in our life.

It is possible for a person to begin to be healed but, as Jesus told in his parable of the sower,[8] for "the cares of this world" to choke out the life of the newly growing plant of health. Consistently caring for others is the herbicide which kills the choking weeds of selfish cares.

How Jesus Serves Us

Jesus taught us the paradoxical truth that we only keep what we give away to others. That makes service not only altruistic but supremely practical. It also assumes that our service is done out of love and not duty. That is why one day every knee shall bow before Jesus[9]—because he, in loving service, bowed before every man. He said that "the Son of man came [out of love—John 3:16] not to be served but to serve" the whole world.[10] His whole life expressed the will to serve others and the sheer delight in living out that attitude. How much of his rich humanity was produced as a return upon his service to others?

Some years ago, a friend who had just experienced the new life and power of the Holy Spirit found himself filled with zeal, love, and joy. He wanted to serve. With deep intensity he shared his desire in a small group.

"I want to go wherever the Lord wants me to go!" he told us. "I want to do whatever Christ wants. Pray that I get clear guidance and understanding as to his mission for my life. When I know for sure, I'll leave everything behind and go out to *serve* him."

The members of the group gathered around him while he knelt, and prayed, "Lord, guide him, direct him. Show him what you want him to do and let him know where you want him to go."

When the prayer was finished, he said he was drawing a blank. He sensed no guidance. We prayed again. This time we simply praised God. We thanked him for what he had done in this man's life. When he opened his eyes, the tears were coursing down his face. Through his tears he said:

"In my mind's eye I saw Jesus walk into the room and kneel in front of me. As he knelt, he said, 'I don't want you to go anywhere or do anything. I just want you to let me serve you.'"

There is a seeming contradiction here. My friend wanted to serve, but he was told not to serve—not yet at least. In his case, that interdiction was psychologically sound. Here was a man who was ready to run out and serve the world. But he had had little experience of selfless service. His service had been done out of duty rather than love. What he needed then was to soak in the beauty of a life which asked nothing but letting Christ serve him and let that experience reconstruct his model of maturity. And he needed time for that model to establish itself in his deepest mind. When that happened, then he was called to serve in the same selfless way. Later he did it as an act of love. Now, several years later, my friend's ministry is known throughout the world. That he was able to allow Jesus to serve him is the primary reason why he has been used so powerfully to serve others.

10.

The Healing Power of
LISTENING

A prominent hostess shared with me this amusing, but ultimately tragic, story.

"I had the most interesting dinner party the other night. One of the women whom I *had* to invite is a pathological, nonstop talker and I was hard put to know where to seat her or what to do with her. After the party she told me she had had the best time she ever had because her dinner partner, a distinguished-looking politician in his sixties, was such an interesting conversationalist. After she told me all of the weighty subjects which 'they' had explored conversationally through the evening, I didn't have the heart to tell her that the man was stone deaf!"

This is a parable of our society which has been conditioned to believe, on the one hand, that talking is communicating, and on the other that because someone is listening to your words, they are understanding what you are saying. Both ideas are danger-ous myths which cause friends to remain strangers and can even lead lovers to become enemies.

Jesus was frequently heard to say, "He who has ears to hear let him hear," because he knew that much of the human tragedy comes from our unwill-ingness to really listen. He referred to the prophets' description of Israel as being like the idols they wor-shiped—having ears but not hearing.[1]

Idolatry is the product of confused values. Today we've eliminated the stone and wooden images, but our idolatries and our confused values still remain. They lead directly to the dehumanized state in which we find ourselves, where we can't hear another person with our hearts. We place huge importance on the in-significant, and tend to relegate to the back shelf of our minds such important qualities as selfless service, compassion and genuine caring. It boils down to the sometimes stated truth of loving things and using people instead of loving people and using things. The only way to move out of this world of the emotionally deaf and dumb is to get ourselves off our own hands. The universal characteristic of the neurotic is that he can't listen to anyone else because he hears only the static created by his own anxieties.

LISTENING BUT NOT HEARING

Seldom does anyone respond in the negative to the question, "Are you a good listener?" Most of us think that we are. What actually happens, though, is that most of the time we take the serious conversation of the significant people close to us—father, mother, sis-ter, brother, intimate—and interpret what is being said in the present by what we have felt in the past.

A wife asks a husband if he would like to go to a movie with her. The husband, hearing the request, also hears an echo of an overbearing, demanding mother of his childhood who insisted he be involved in youth activities of her choosing, and who was constantly insisting his father go with her in a dizzy round of social events, when he frequently wanted to stay home and work in his shop. Unconscious of his anger over his mother's past control, he is deaf to the real request his wife is making now. She wants to be alone with him, away from the pressures of domestic demands. All he hears is the nagging demand of a wife whom he has changed into his mother.

A teacher in a classroom calls a student to her desk. She asks him why he hasn't done his assignments for the last six weeks. "You're a good student," she says, "but if you continue to neglect your homework, I'm going to have to fail you."

The boy glares at her and says, "I don't give a damn what you do."

The teacher exclaims, "Don't talk to me like that!"

What the teacher missed was that the boy was crying for help. She had been conditioned by her parents' attitudes to believe that academic excellence was a primary evidence of personal superiority. They had always praised her for her good grades and sternly criticized her or implied their displeasure when she wasn't one of the best in the class in a given examination. This conditioning made her meet her failing student on the wrong level—that of grades and classroom success.

If she had met him on the level of personal emotional concern, she might have asked him, "Has anything happened at home in your personal life which made you give up on your school work?" Because this is exactly what had happened. Six weeks earlier, his parents had separated after a drunken brawl, which he had witnessed. The whole ugly episode crushed him, leaving him confused and angry at the world, and robbing him of any will to achieve.

These examples of listening but not hearing have one thing in common. The emotional inadequacy of the listeners made them insensitive to the affective message being sent by the one they thought they were hearing. Through inner healing the auditory blockage may be removed.

LISTENING TO GOD

Although inner healing of the unconscious mind is essential for the refinement of our ability to sense the hurt in others and to provide the kind of empathetic listening which heals, the rediscovery of the spiritual dimension of communication is the first and most basic step. That means learning to listen to God.

The seldom-considered art of listening to God is learned as we bring ourselves to the place of attentive silence. Because as human beings we need silence, and because our noisy Christianity tends to ignore that need, into that void has rushed a variety of Eastern meditative disciplines, the most popular of which is Transcendental Meditation. There is no need to argue against such disciplines. What we need is to discover the authentic native Christian expression of meditation which makes all other disciplines unnecessary and inferior.

What really is needed is the reeducation of our hearts. Our radio, television, and motion picture approach to communication makes us tend to believe that silence is something which should be filled with sound. Silence intimidates when it should bless. It is looked upon as a void, when it could and should be considered a profound opportunity for communication with God. Fish who live in the darkness of underground caves have lost the capacity to use their eyes. In the same way we who have been unwilling, through ignorance, to live in the light of silence have lost the ability to exercise that divinely bestowed sixth sense which enables us to listen in meditation to the voiceless voice of God.

For those who wish to rediscover the gift of meditation, certain simple rules must be followed. They may seem difficult, foreign, and unproductive at first. So does reaching down to touch your toes if you have neglected physical exercise for a long time. But the strange will prove very healthy and natural with a little patience and perseverance.

WHEN TO MEDITATE

The best times to meditate, at first, are in the morning, before any activity has begun, and in the early evening, before supper. These are the two times of day when, according to scientific research, vitality is at its lowest ebb. The ultimate goal is to be able to meditate at any time. That means we should be able to draw down the curtain of our mind at will, blocking out the insignificant activities of life, and focusing on the throne room of the soul where God dwells, and listening for his voice.

Since we are creatures of habit, it is far more beneficial to set aside a brief period of five minutes in each day than to undertake prolonged effort (a half hour to an hour) once a week. The longer periods tend to discourage and fatigue the beginner in meditation. Faithfulness in the brief moments of daily meditation will bring natural growth toward longer periods after the pattern has been well established.

THE PLACE OF MEDITATION

It is best to select a quiet and isolated place, free from family traffic. It is helpful to have a lock on the door, especially when you first undertake the discipline of meditation. The reason for this is that if there is any likelihood that someone could break in on your meditation, the unconscious mind will tend to remain tense and on guard.

All you need is a chair in which you can sit with spine erect and your back away from the back of the chair. Your head too should be erect.

It is possible, also, to lie on a flat, firm surface with no pillow under the head. The only problem with this position is that if you are at all fatigued, you may fall asleep.

MOVING INTO MEDITATION

There are three parts or steps to meditation. They are preparation, concentration, and meditation itself. In the initial period of preparation, the body, the temple of the Holy Spirit, must be made ready. Anxiety and tension are the enemies of effective meditation. Mild physical exercise can relieve both. A warm shower or tub bath, taken in a spirit of cleansing and worship, is beneficial. As you wash you can thank Jesus Christ for cleansing and purifying your life, and for washing away all troubles that have soiled your spirit.

Then the mind must be prepared. Read some of your favorite devotional material, such as *God Call-*

ing or *Streams in the Desert.* Or read a Psalm. Conclude with a brief reading from the life of Jesus out of one of the Gospels.

Finally, the soul must be prepared. Enter into a brief period of prayer. Repeat the Lord's Prayer or extemporaneously ask the Holy Spirit to bless this divine exercise.

At last, seated or lying down, use your breath as an expression of inspiration. Notice how Jesus used his breath to express spiritual blessing to the disciples. "He breathed on them, and said to them, 'Receive the Holy Spirit.' "[2] Breathing in preparation for meditation reflects this kind of understanding of its spiritual nature. Breathe in deeply before meditation, repeating in your mind as you breathe, "I breathe in the Spirit," and exhaling saying, "I breathe out love." Repeat this breathing cycle five or six times.

The final preparatory step is concentration. Through concentration, our minds become incredibly more powerful, as a light ray does when it is focused through a ruby crystal to become a laser beam. Laser beams can cut through a thick steel plate in seconds, and flash a decipherable message from earth to the surface of the moon, to mention just a few of their versatile and powerful uses. The concentrated mind is more amazing. It can become a vehicle for communicating with the core of our being which Jesus called "the kingdom of God within." It can cut through thick mental barriers erected to wall pain out which end up walling God out, too.

To achieve this concentration, select a single meaningful phrase such as, "I am one with God," "God is love" or just the word *Jesus* or *God.* With your eyes closed, quietly and slowly, begin to repeat this phrase or word over and over in your mind (not audibly). If yours is the average experience, in a short while your mind will begin to drift away from the phrase. Don't be discouraged. Don't try to fight the drift of your mind. Quietly, but firmly, return to the phrase you have chosen. Make no effort to move beyond this repetition because when you are ready, you will automatically flow into that indescribable, indefinable state of mind we call meditation.

INNER HEALING THROUGH MEDITATION

How does meditation pertain to inner healing? One problem in finding emotional healing is the fear of facing our emotional problems. Or if we have faced them too frequently, we don't want others to see them, we are afraid to share them, lest we be rejected. In the experience of meditation, a slow, subtle change occurs in our personal focus. Normally a disturbed or neurotic person is tortured by the pain created by emotional imbalance. The nature of the problem is obscured because heavy unconscious effort is invested into hiding from it, making it difficult to deal with it.

For instance, if we feel the compulsive need to criticize others or to berate ourselves, it usually isn't at all clear why this condition exists or how the pattern can be eliminated. And the more we worry and fret about it, the more likely it will be that personal frustration will increase and the chance of solution will diminish. In meditation, the focus changes from doing to being. Whether one is whole or broken, the focus turns away from one's emotional condition to spiritual reality.

As meditation begins, the heart is tuned to listen to truth it consciously would deny, such as the repeated phrase, "God is love," or "I am one with God," or "Jesus is Lord." The heart may want to shut itself up and not hear. But when one quietly, persistently repeats such truth, the moment comes sooner or later when the unconscious can no longer resist. It quietly sits and listens to the mind's affirmation of what the soul deeply knows. Two things then occur. In the midst of the meditation, peace envelops the whole of the person. Now we are dwelling "in the secret place of the most High" and abiding "under the shadow of the Almighty."[3]

In this state of being, we aren't escaping from problems but, literally, there are no problems. A second benefit occurs when one is near but not in the state of meditation. Frequently, the Holy Spirit is able to illumine any formerly insoluble problem as the mind is quieted. A childhood moment may be vividly recalled, an unforgiven guilt of the past, an emotional disappointment, or a tragedy which had been buried alive may surface. It is as though the soul enters a region in which Christ dwells. There every problem of life can receive solutions and answers from Christ. But before that answer can be given the mind to apply, the inner child of the heart must cooperate. It must give its approval. And before that can happen, it must become quiet enough to listen and hear. A by-product of meditation is such listening quietude.

CREATIVE WAITING

It is important to know how to wait quietly for God to work. Sensitivity to God's direction is more important than activity in finding emotional solutions, and that can only come by taking time to listen. Our society tells us that if we want something done we should go out and do it. But on the road to wholeness, the heeding of such advice can lead to painful wastes of time.

Arlene related a story of her inner healing which underscores the importance of waiting, listening, and letting the Spirit take the initiative.

Arlene had known from her earliest years that she was adopted. This created an identity crisis and feelings of rejection which tormented her. What she did not know until her later years was that she was the illegitimate daughter of her adoptive father and that her biological mother had died in childbirth.

Excerpts from a recent letter show how she was able to deal with this emotional blight:

"A large part of my life has been spent feeling that I belonged to two people I could never know. The teenage years went by, painful and empty, without the discovery that I felt would give meaning to my identity."

Though a beautiful woman, Arlene had a brutally low opinion of herself. An early marriage ended in divorce after four children. At this point, as she describes it, "I reached out to the only being I knew who could possibly love me, Jesus Christ.

"There had been several childhood years that as an adult were blocked from my memory. An old family maid had come to nurse me during a time of recuperation from major surgery. I asked her if she could tell me anything about my childhood."

It was then Arlene discovered that she was the illegitimate child of her adoptive father, and that she was often treated brutally during his frequent drunken binges. She continued her story, "This knowledge ended my search for the identity of my father, but did not reveal who my mother was. In prayer I asked God, 'What about my mother?' His answer came swiftly: 'In my own time and in a way you will recognize, I will reveal her to you.'"

Several months after an inner healing workshop, she experienced dreadful but healing recall: infant memories of parental violence.

"A month after this experience," she continued, "I injured my foot and although I felt well, I was in bed for several days to keep my foot elevated. Shortly after noon on the second day, alone, in silence, I became sleepy. I was taking no medication. I closed my eyes and seconds afterwards a form began to appear before my eyes. As it resolved into the face of a young woman, I knew instantly that this was my natural mother. I was filled with a warmth I had never known existed. I felt secure, loved, and whole in the moments the face stayed there. For the first time in thirty-seven years I really belonged.

"This happened months ago, yet I still carry the feelings of that experience.

"Recently it has come to me that I was conceived in drunkenness. I feel that this is the root cause of the lingering guilt and shame I've borne all my life. Yet, I know with my whole being that through inner healing Christ's love will bring me into wholeness. I am no longer afraid."

If this woman had sought to find her identity by scouring records or interviewing friends and relatives, she might have been able to uncover some shadowy facts and statistics about the mother she longed to know. But by listening to the inner guidance and waiting for God's time to reveal this woman, she was able to experience a spiritual reunion with her. Somehow she knew her. She experienced a mother's love and caring which gave birth to an inner peace she had never known.

LISTENING VERSUS STRUGGLING

Most people could never identify with the experience described by this woman. But the principle of waiting on God is valid for all. It is important to understand that God speaks to us through our thoughts and experiences. If frustration torments us, if we can't find an immediate solution to our emotional dilemma, it may be that God is saying, "Stop struggling I have the answer for you, but you must trust me to bring it to you in my time and my way."

One alternative is to struggle more intensely. But struggling can be like tying a knot in a water hose and then wondering why the water won't flow out. To stop struggling, to abandon effort into the hands of God, enables us to relax. This, in a sense, unties the knot, allowing the flow to begin. By letting the tension of struggle go slack, creative thought and insight begin to flow.

The case of Frances illustrates the importance of the quiet spirit. She deeply loved her husband. But buried within was something which made her pathologically suspicious of him. An earlier experience had shaken her trust in him. She blamed her suspicion on his confession of infidelity. But years later, she still found herself unable to forgive and forget. She was constantly tormented by suspecting various infidelities with other women. She tried everything she knew, counseling, confession, further introspection, but nothing succeeded. Her torment and love walked hand in hand.

One day her husband said to her he could stand her jealousy and outbursts no more. He submitted the ultimatum that she either deal with the issue or their marriage would have to be terminated. He could no longer stand the pain of being the cause of her agony while doing nothing to create it.

Then she determined she had to find the source of her pain. Clearly they had run out of answers. There was nowhere to turn except to God. Either he would give the answer or a couple who loved each other would be pried apart by a state of mind neither could understand. In emotional fatigue, they withdrew from the conflict with one another and began quietly to wait on the Lord.

One evening after her husband had retired, sleep kept eluding him. As he lay in bed restlessly tossing, he whispered to God, "Please show me what is wrong. Why is Frances going through needless torment?"

The answer came, "It is not needless. To remove the pain from her before the cause is removed would be cruel."

Then came a series of insights about this woman he so deeply loved. He took a pad and pen and began to write. Addressing the note to her, he outlined her emotional history. He reminded her how her father, a wealthy industrialist, had focused almost all his emotional attention on her. She had revealed to him her jealousy of anyone in the family who attempted to relate intimately with her father, even her mother: she had compulsively lied, and unconsciously manipulated everyone to maintain her father's approval. Her father responded by showering her with excessive attention which confirmed to her inner child that the two things needed for happiness were to be number one in all situations and to have a daddy's constant care.

When Frances read the note, she knew it contained reasons why her jealousies were constant. Any time her husband left her sight, he was no longer able to shower attention on her. This filled her with a sense of threat. She was losing her daddy. This attitude caused the most harmless and benign relationships in her husband's life to appear threatening to her.

That evening she sat on the bed beside him and asked God to release her from this egocentric trap. She no longer wanted to remain a child. She wanted to move toward a maturity which would allow her husband to be free and her to be free of torment.

She discovered that even to pray it required determination. She knew the process was not completed with that prayer, but that the pain of overcoming the future moments when she would find herself reverting to the old pattern would be far more bearable than the corrosive effect of her past jealousies. She willed to overcome and with this new insight she knew she could.

Her breakthrough came when they stopped listening to one another's angry recriminations and started listening to God. One way to implement Jesus' words, "Seek and ye shall find," well could be, "Quietly listen and you shall hear."

LISTENING TO THE FAMILIAR

The discussion of the art of listening has been kept so far at the rather high altitude of meditation and spiritual release. And these heavens do declare the glory of God. But so do a lot of earthly, more humble things. God speaks in autumn leaves, in a baby's smile, in birds and flowers, in songs, dance and art. We need to learn to use such familiar things to tune out our pain and tune in the voice and love of God.

This is what Jesus was suggesting when he said,

"Look at the birds of the air. . . . Consider the lilies of the field." He was giving us an antidote for anxiety.[4] If we could really sense what God was saying in his creation, that every need of life is anticipated and provided for by the heavenly Father, we would not worry about monthly bills, we would not be frustrated about taxes or worry about being taken advantage of by unscrupulous repairmen. We would see an end to our hand-wringing anxiety over the health of our children or even the dangers of a thermonuclear world. We have much to learn about God's care, Jesus was saying, by looking at and listening to God's creation. Heaven and earth are full of his glory.

Cases of deep depression find the natural world a helpful resource in inner healing. If you are the one out of each six people who experiences deep depression, you know how impossible it is to heed such well-meaning advice as "Just praise God in the midst of your depression" or "All you need to do is pray about it." What a depressive finds it nearly impossible to do in the emotional darkness is praise or pray. Sometimes, to attempt it sets up internal reactions that tend to deepen the depression. I have heard depressives say, "Since I cannot pray or praise, I must be utterly God-forsaken."

One thing can and does speak to a despondent person. A walk in the woods or, for someone in the city, a stroll in the nearest park, even in the rain or snow, can help to loose the grip of utter despair. Physical exercise, to some, may not seem like a spiritual activity, but it can be God's chosen therapy. Anything to get closer to nature can help integrate your spirit, put things in perspective, or simply soothe your mind, so that deeper healing can begin.

Of the available wide variety of therapeutic natural beauties, take advantage of what seems to be most suited to your temperament. And always be prepared for the exception which tests this rule. Some will be guided by the Spirit to an experience which has seemed totally foreign to their past history. The indoor bookworm may take up strenuous muscular exercise, the outdoor athletic type may find a fresh perspective in the music of Brahms.

One woman tells of what a day at the shore did for her. She had been told by her physicians that she was dying of inoperable cancer, and had only a few months to live. There was nothing more medical skill could do for her. Driving to a beach alone, she sought some peace of mind in the ocean beauty she loved so much. Lying on the beach, she found herself caught up in the rhythm of nature: the waves breaking in cadence upon the shore, the wind blowing through the leaves of a nearby tree created a tempo that seemed to be to her the heartbeat of the universe. Quite unexpectedly, she felt a surge of power framed in joy flow through her. At the moment, she thought it was merely a sense of ecstasy over the beauty of the seascape. But as the days proceeded, she realized that all the symptoms of her disease were gone. The earth had become the catalyst of her healing. What scalpels and medication couldn't touch, Christ, in sea and wind, did.

LISTENING TO THE POSITIVE

Just as our physical bodies benefit from proper nourishment and exercise, so do our minds. I mean that what we feed into our minds today in terms of emotional experience and thought will, in great measure, determine our emotional health or illness tomorrow. This is the principle of sowing and reaping. Paul wrote to the Galatian Christians, "Do not be deceived; God is not mocked, for whatever a man sows, that he will also reap."[5]

As Christians, we have been so blessed with our understanding of God's grace, his total forgiveness, that we are sometimes lulled into believing it "cheap grace," to use Dietrich Bonhoeffer's term. We sometimes neglect our responsibility to fill our minds with the good and the beautiful rather than the ugly, the trashy, the unworthy. And then we think that at any given time we should be able to draw upon the inner voice of God because God loves us. This ignores his principle of sowing and reaping.

Those who daily fill their minds with thoughts of love for God and others, who learn to smile so that others may be happy without intending to impress others with their humor or piety, are quietly building a storehouse of blessing which will enable them to hear and heed the voice of God.

Stability and balance come as naturally as breathing when one is careful day after day to sow the seeds of creative and positive thought.

Some years ago I read of a discipline which helped me correct thought patterns that would inevitably lead to needless emotional pain. The author called this discipline "a spiritual fast." It involved an abstinence, not from physical food, but from negative food for thought. For a period of seven days one seeks to be obedient to the scriptural instruction, "Whatever is true, whatever is honorable, whatever is just, whatever is pure, whatever is lovely, whatever is gracious, if there is any excellence, if there is anything worthy of praise, think about these things."[6] The instruction was to press gently out of one's mind any negative thoughts which might appear and replace them with positive thoughts.

At first, it seems to be a constitutional impossibility to manipulate thoughts that way, but with a little practice and a lot of determination, it begins to work. I had one overwhelming negative thought when I first began this exercise. That was the appalling discovery of how many negative thoughts filled my mind!

Although this can be an unnatural discipline leaning toward the pollyanna, it does act as a corrective. It allows us to "bring down every deceptive fantasy and every imposing defense that [we] erect against the true knowledge of God. We even fight to capture every thought until it acknowledges the authority of Christ."[7] It also enables one to maintain, in the face of adversity, the mental balance necessary to hear the healing, helping voice of God. Such an "ounce of prevention" approach is basic in growth toward real emotional and spiritual maturity.

11.

The Healing Power of
ADVERSITY

One characteristic found in most great people is pain, adversity and injury *overcome*. Helen Keller, Mahatma Gandhi, David Livingstone, Anne Frank, to name only a very few, are honored because they had a spiritual stature which rose like a phoenix out of the ashes of adversity and was, in fact, formed by the same ugly forces which disfigured and crushed others.

Since pain is a part of every person's experience, we would do well to learn how to deal with this emotional gargoyle It is possible to experience healing through injury and pain without assistance from anyone and without any other tool being used. It is helpful, however, to know that there are stages through which we can travel from pain to peace.

STATIONS OF OUR CROSSES

In her study of the experience of dying, Dr. Elizabeth Kübler-Ross discovered that dying people go through various emotional stages. When first told that they are dying, they deny it. Then anger and fear set in. In the next stage they bargain with God—"If you let me live, I'll do or be such and such . . ." This is followed by dark depression, and finally by the emotion of resignation and acceptance of the inevitability of death.

There is a similar path for any who face the frustration of pain or any bitter crushing of life. At any point along these stations of our personal cross-bearing, the pain of the problem can cause a transformation. It can become the meeting place between the Lord of Life and our broken self. But the final step, acceptance, can never be omitted.

Usually when confronted with "the slings and arrows of outrageous fortune," we have a tendency to deny our problem. The denial will not be direct. That is, we do not say, "I'm not blind in one eye," if in fact we are, or "My wife hasn't left me," if she has. Only the psychotic personality can so totally deny reality. That, in fact, is the function of emotional withdrawal or fantasy in the deeply troubled. It allows them to cope with pain they no longer can face. But what identifies them most clearly as insane—their uncreative, sick denial of reality—is in more subtle form at the heart of the average person's ineffective living. Our denials take the less obvious form of escape or rationalization. We use our limitation as an excuse instead of a challenge. It is difficult to believe that adversity is only an enemy when we choose to fight it. But that is the truth. Accepted and then embraced, it becomes our servant. But denying it, running from it is the common, human, corrupting response.

DEATH THROUGH A BIRTH

Recently, I sat across from a couple who had just become the grandparents of their daughter's baby, born out of wedlock. They knew nothing of the joy I experienced when my daughter made me the grandmother of a beautiful baby girl. I could not let a day go by without visiting that precious, angelic child. I felt like a mother all over again. I had forgotten how much I loved babies and the maternal role. Grandmotherhood may be more like eating out at a restaurant than cooking in one's own kitchen—it is easier and less fulfilling—but it is a joy.

This couple told me of the shock they experienced when they first learned of their daughter's pregnancy. In the beginning, they refused to believe that their child could have gotten herself into such a mess. They tried to convince themselves that it was only a daughter's frightened response to a moment of immoral indiscretion. Surely their daughter was not pregnant, they insisted. They almost got to the place where they felt that if they ignored it, it would go away. But it would not. And their suffering grew unbearable.

Just as in facing dying, anger followed denial. The father especially was angry at the daughter for humiliating and disobeying him. She was a rebel, and he resented that she at last had succeeded in doing what to him was the most degrading thing a young lady could do. But his out-of-control emotions made him face himself. He considered himself a Christian of some stature, and he could not hide from the fact that his response to his child's plight was neither loving nor understanding.

It was obvious to him that his reaction to his daughter's plight was disproportionate to the deed—he was overreacting. He knew that his attitude should be loving, consoling and empathetic. But how could he attain this attitude when everything within him was screaming with anger and outrage? His need for deep healing was compelling, but he did not know how to respond to it.

For weeks he struggled with his anger and his daughter's dilemma. The only thing that seemed to lessen his bitterness was the hope that maybe she could redeem the situation. The young sire had made clear that he did not want to marry his pregnant girlfriend. She bitterly said she was not about to marry a mindless child like him. He had used her and then bailed out.

This second stage was a time in which counseling could have speeded the father's inner healing. But he didn't seek counseling. Instead, he began to pray, "God, let her meet someone who wants to marry her, or let her have a miscarriage, and I'll give her the attention I know she wants from me." Following the same emotional process at work in confronting physical death, he had lapsed into the let's-make-a-deal-with-God level: "If you'll get my daughter out of this, I'll serve you as never before. Please, let a man marry my daughter so the baby will have parents and my daughter can be its mother. I'll do anything you ask if you'll only redeem this terrible situation."

God Makes All the Concessions

Of course, there is no creative power, no spiritual integrity in such deal-making. God will not let us bargain our way into his kingdom. We always want to reduce God to our own petty passions. The degraded deities who lived in Grecian myth on Mt. Olympus perverting and corrupting each other and mortal men are only the extreme expression of what we still do to the sublime God revealed by Jesus Christ. All of our lives we have watched our parents and the adult world try to strike bargains, negotiate tit-for-tat in order to gain some desired advantage. So it seems to any conditioned subconscious only reasonable to imagine that God has this same mentality. But this is to make God in our image. Christ, on the contrary, died to heal this illusion and to enable us to see that we are created in the image of a God who is love. He is no God-father making us frightening deals we can't refuse. He is our Father God who wants only our well-being and wholeness.

He makes all the concessions to enable us to realize this relationship. But often such a realization takes place only after the pressure of continued pain. And if it does, he would not destroy the opportunities in creative crisis by responding to a bargain we may offer him. When the situations of life get ugly, and more particularly, when we get emotionally ugly and it begins to dawn on us that nothing we can do will increase God's willingness to help, that his will to bless us is already total, the crisis has done its job. There are few lessons in life which are harder to learn or, once learned, more enabling. God requires only that we accept and appropriate the absolute love which is always and completely available.

So the bargaining prayer of the distraught father was not answered. No husband for his daughter appeared. No miscarriage took place. She just got more and more pregnant and he grew more miserable. He became terribly depressed. But such depression is one half of an equation for healing. The despair of feeling that you have no solution to a problem needs only to have added to it the fact that God does have the solution. At this point his misery was so intense that he was a perfect candidate for inner healing. Still his resistance was too great.

An Equation for Resolution

Despair plus faith equals resolution of the problem. This is why Jesus said, "Blessed are the poor in spirit."[1] The poor in spirit know that they have nothing but God to sustain their lives. It is the first of the Beatitudes because it is essential to emotional wholeness and spiritual survival. We grow up with the myth that the race is won by the swift, the battle by the bold and the able. And, of course, there is an element of truth in this myth. But ultimately only God maintains us through every hour of life, and only God sustains us in the hour of death. Death simply exposes a human dependence on God which every previous moment should have acknowledged. "In [God] we live and move and have our being," wrote St. Paul quoting a Greek poet.[2] It sometimes requires pain or desperation to learn that (1) I have nothing. (2) God has everything. (3) God's abundant supply is available to me.

By itself, the I-have-nothing proposition is a poverty complex which can never give anyone anything but a sense of defeat and despair. The opposite attitude, "I have everything; I'm the greatest," may encourage a person to win a few more laurels in life. But there is the smell of pettiness and death about such an attitude. It frankly lacks balance, and in the long run will bankrupt us at the time we need God the most. This kind of self-confidence is filled with ultimate defeat because it cuts us off from the Source of life.

My own early life flourished in this fantasy. I was a beautiful child with long, blond curly hair. I was the apple of my father's eye. I was raised among black children who treated me like the heir-apparent to my father's throne. I was sure I was the greatest. I needed no course in self-improvement. I was "it." It took inner healing to allow me to discover how blessed I was when I had my rude, cruel awakening that I was not the most lovely and loved woman in the land.

A person called me recently who was busy making her life as busy as possible. She is in perpetual motion—coming, going, crusading and parading her hollow importance. I can't judge her. I know where she is because I have been there. I fought to maintain a trembling hold on sanity by being the busiest woman in town. When I finished talking with my similarly cursed friend, I could read her sad signals only too easily. She can't afford to get quiet. There is a little child deep within her screaming for help. If she stops her hectic pace she will hear that child once again. And it is easier to keep up the discotheque din of activity than to listen to her troubled heart.

But she is going to run out of noisemakers pretty soon, just as I did. Then she will be forced to listen and to learn that only God is the source of life's satisfaction. She probably would say, "I know that already." Her life style says that she knows it with her intellect but neither her heart nor her inner child are convinced.

Pain is the great persuader. The psalmist wrote, "The eternal God is our refuge." Those are lovely and true words. But the only person who ever seeks a refuge is someone on the run, a fugitive, a person fleeing from threat. "And underneath are the everlasting arms," the psalmist concludes.[3] No one cares about divine arms as long as they believe human arms are strong enough to sustain them. So the arm-weary refugees from the ravages of unhappiness, sorrow, disappointment are prime candidates for the blessing of those who are poor in spirit *if* (and that is a crucial *if*) they know that God cares. That is the last part of this spiritual success formula—and the most difficult to realize. God's help is most often sought when a person "bottoms out." From this point on, inner healing can begin the process of purification. We can often look back and see that pain was the purifier.

SLOW DEATH

Sometimes the emotional death process can be very slow. The father of the unwed mother had to suffer through great depression and despondency before he reached acceptance and that sublime inner vision. Quite suddenly he broke through despair into a new consciousness. He died to some unidentified emotional flaw. He left the corpse of an old mentality when he recognized his injury as blessing. By the time his grandson was born, he had nothing but love for it and its mother.

The daughter chose to put the baby up for adoption. It was painful to say goodbye to the little fellow. He asked if he and his wife could bring the baby home for a few hours. The authorities said that he could. He stood holding the baby he once abhorred and wept in love and blessing. He prayed that the Spirit would bless the couple which was to take the baby to their home the next day, that they would be given the love and wisdom to raise it properly. As he put his tiny grandson back in the basinette, he knew he had been born again to a new level of life through his grandson.

Nine months may seem interminable to one who is suffering from deep injury, but I once knew a man who went through agonies of hell for over three decades before he experienced inner healing.

I was seated in the back of the auditorium where I was to speak to an interdenominational Christian conference, when a short, stout, elderly man sat down beside me and smiled at me cautiously. When I asked him what group he was with, he responded, "Oh, I'm not one of these people. I'm not even a Christian. I'm here because I had a strange experience the other night." He had awakened, he said, in the middle of the night and heard a voice speak out of nowhere. *Jesus Christ,* it said in a quiet, reverent tone.

"I thought it was my imagination and went back to sleep. But something roused me again. And I heard the words again, *Jesus Christ.*" The strange invisible herald was still branded as imagination by the man—until it happened a third time. He didn't know what to do, but felt he'd better investigate. He had never taken Jesus seriously as anything more than the historical founder of one of the great religions of the world. He prided himself on being a student of world religions. But the voice in the night made him wonder if there was not more to Jesus than he had thought. Seeing the advertisement for the meeting, he had decided to attend.

It wasn't long after he had defensively explained why he was present that I was called up to the podium to speak. I had not told him that I was the speaker. And he later said he would have been surprised to discover this, except that he was overwhelmed when he learned that months before, I had been asked to speak on the single theme, "Jesus Christ." During my speech, I had no idea at the end of each point what the next point would be. But always it turned out to be an unfolding exposition of Jesus Christ and his unconditional love.

As the session opened the following morning, there was my little old friend in the back row. He had not been scared away. At the afternoon session there he was again. He smiled as he walked in and waved at me. I waved back. "I'm hanging in there," he seemed to be saying to me.

After the final message on the third day many people came to me for individual counseling. One of the first was the short, stout man. He stared at me through tear-filled eyes with a look of hope and fear. We sat down together and he said, "Mrs. Stapleton, I have never heard Jesus Christ described in this way. I need his help and you make me think he can help me." Then he told a strange and tragic story.

Over three decades before, he had saved enough money to take a boat to a foreign land. He had made arrangements to go to work for a resort hotel. After a long sea voyage and a bus trip, he arrived at the hotel where he was promised employment. This had been his teenage dream. But the dream was short-lived. The hotel manager said he would get no salary, just room and board for scrubbing floors, bussing tables, and lighting the furnace each morning. Bitterly he decided that there was no future in this servitude. So, he decided that after completing his first night's chores and lighting the furnace the next morning, he would return home.

Before dawn he had his bag of meager belongings packed. He went down to the furnace room where he had been shown the day before how to start up the bank of burners. He had never seen anything so modern in his life.

Part of the burners ignited, but for some reason the others would not go on. What was operating seemed to be functioning well, so he turned them up as far as they would go. Then he went up to his room, grabbed his worn brown suitcase with a rope tied around it, headed out the door and down the road to a main highway which he knew would take him back the way he came.

He was about a half a block from the hotel when he heard a huge explosion. Looking back he saw the hotel engulfed in flames, smoke billowing from its broken windows. For a few seconds he gazed at the inferno. Then he fled, not daring to look back again.

He told me that he had been running from that fire ever since. He had never learned the toll in lives and property. But the nightmare had haunted him for over thirty years.

"Do you think Christ can forgive me for what I did?"

"He did two thousand years ago," I assured him. "That is what the cross is all about. Jesus took your guilt on himself so that you never have to carry any guilt—ever! In the name of Jesus Christ you are absolved of all guilt. When Christ died on the cross, he had taken on himself all guilt that you have suffered under."

The man broke into deep sobs. He knew I was telling him the truth. After weeping out feelings that had been strangling him for so many years, he looked up at me, his reddened eyes aglow. A new smile framed his bulky face. "It's gone," he said. Before I could ask what was gone, he added, "The lump in my throat I've had since the day of the explosion. It's completely gone." Also gone were the guilt and the grief which caused it.

The significant fact is that there came a moment of knowing and release to this desperate long-term seeker. The process of removing all the retardant to the flame of the Spirit in his soul had taken better than a quarter of a century. At last he was ready to die to whatever unconsciously had blocked his spiritual vision. He had been looking at facts about Jesus for a long time. But he had been unable to see him until his heart had been purified. It was not my presentation which made the difference. An invisible spokesman for Christ spoke his name to this man as soon as he was ready to hear. The response of the seeker to the voice in the night is further proof that his heart was ready to enter any door even if his intellect had to humble itself. When it did become teachable, this short little man walked tall into the kingdom of God.

THE SMASHING OF IDOLS

Eldridge Cleaver's story of his conversion reveals the same principle of purification and healing through pain. His illusion was that he could build a brave new world through violence. He worshiped the wrong gods. His demigod heroes were Mao Tsetung and Fidel Castro. As the foremost advocate of black violence in America, he had a Samsonlike determination in his blind rage against whites to bring the temple of freedom down on his own head. But it is important to consider, in retrospect, that he was just as sincere as St. Paul was in his violence-ridden preconversion days. In his classic commentary on black rage in white America, *Soul on Ice*, Cleaver told it like it is for the spiritually destitute, culturally humiliated black American. But he was completely out of touch with the spiritual genius of men like George Washington Carver or Martin Luther King. They are the real black freedom fighters. And they never used violence. They are the heirs of the spirit found in the old spiritual which says, "Nobody knows the trouble I've seen . . . Glory, hallelujah." Out of the soul of slaves who had been freed by sorrow given to God, came this paradox of praise in pain: "trouble . . ." to "glory . . ."

Cleaver began at the right place—with trouble, lots of it. What he did not know was that the men he most respected would prove to be tragic troublemakers and not creative revolutionaries. His brief residence in Cuba showed him Castro's tyranny. In Algeria, he saw another police state which he grew to hate with increasing passion. In his search for truth, the agony of discovering that his heroes had feet of clay, bloody hands, and often empty heads left his "certainties" in shambles. Old dogmas, angry posturing, no longer satisfied him.

It was in this climate that Cleaver started reading Thoreau, Gandhi, and King. In Martin Luther King's writings he noted the frequent reference to Jesus.

Pursuing this lead, he began to read about Jesus in the Gospels.

The ancients said, "When the pupil is ready, the teacher will come." This was a primitive understanding that God's universe is always ready to give truth to the seeker once the heart is prepared to receive it. "Do not throw your pearls before swine," Jesus instructed.[4] I don't think he was prejudiced against pigs. He simply knew that pigs put a high value on garbage and no value on pearls. Some people are like that, he was saying. Place a truth before them and they will trample on it, trying to get to the garbage they so relish. Until this time the black revolutionary would have trampled on the pearls of truth.

As Eldridge Cleaver began to read about Jesus, he was ready. It would have been foolish to try to convert him before he fled this country and faced his fallen shattered idols. As long as he thought Fidel or Mao could rebuild the world, there was no room for Jesus Christ.

THE DANGER OF CUSHIONING OUR CHILDREN'S FALLS

This should comfort the parents who see their child running to the soiled earthen idols of wealth, sensuality, fame or emotional hoboism. It should be remembered that these deities quickly weather and crumble in the heat and storms of life. We do God a disservice when we try to protect our adolescent children from necessary pain. Because, in time, sin is always painful. It dries the human spirit like the Sahara. And if anyone thinks that anything can be a substitute for the love of Christ and commitment to him, it would be wise for the person to go with total abandon into the illusory pleasure they seek. If the quest for life in the valley of dry bones is undertaken diligently enough, the pleasure will quickly pall and the redeeming pain of disillusionment and thirst for satisfaction will dry their soul. Such pain is God's opportunity.

That was Cleaver's condition as he read about Jesus. At the end of his bitter disenchantment with violent revolution, he had experienced the unconscious purging of much of the hate which made the likes of Jesus repugnant. He described the peak experience in his transformation in mystical terms.

He was lying on the ground one night looking up at the moon. Across the orb of the full moon passed the faces of those prominant revolutionaries he had made his heroes. Then there appeared the face of Jesus, and with it came a consuming sense of peace. He knew in that moment what the sincere seeker always will find—that the meek inherit the earth and that the carpenter from Nazareth is the one who alone holds the blueprint for rebuilding broken lives and a substandard world.

It really should not seem strange to a follower of Jesus to learn that pain and suffering can heal. He died on a cross. And that was the act which heals any who embrace it.

12.

The Healing Power of
AUTHENTIC SELF-IDENTITY

I am a unique person. And so are you. With all the similarities which disguise this uniqueness—stereotype clothing, male and female body design and functions, minds which seem to have been similarly programmed—each of us is totally unique.

The discovery of that rich individuality is one of Christ's goals for us. But it is one I had never considered until after I became a speaker and conference leader. When I had my conversion experience and discovered who Jesus was, I thought that I automatically knew who I was. That was a rash assumption. And it was not until my emotional life started to unravel that I faced my sad ignorance about me.

A speaker at a religious conference I was attending asked us, "If you could have your hearts' desire, what would it be?" I sat in the silence which followed and thought, "That's easy. I want to be more like Jesus."

I had no more than finished my lovely thought when the speaker instructed, "Now, don't say, 'I want to be more like Jesus.'"

I was disturbed by his impiety until he explained why such a response could hamper our quest for fulfillment. He had gone through a period, he said, when he was utterly driven by the desire to "save the whole, wide world." In the midst of this zealous crusade, someone asked him the question he had just put to us. And he was stunned to realize that he did not really know what he wanted or needed in his life. He had to confess to himself that he was out of touch with the needs of his own heart. He had smothered his own spirit with a blanket of busyness. He was out there trying to bring to others what they needed—the love, joy, and peace of Christ—and had ignored that he was a person who had needs.

His words struck a chord of deep discontent in me. When I returned home, I started to ask myself why I could not satisfactorily answer the question, "What do I need, really need and want in my life?" I knew I needed something more. But why could I not identify it? And why was I so tormented by this question?

A Person versus a Role

The anxiety became so unbearable that I sought the counsel of a friend who was pastor of a local church. Seated before him in his study I heard him say, "Tell me all about yourself." I proceeded to tell him about my Christian service, my experience as a wife and mother. I delighted in doing so for an entire hour. When I concluded, he responded by saying, "Now tell me about you."

"I just did."

"No," he insisted, "you haven't told me about you. You described three roles you play as a Christian, as a wife, and as a mother; I want to know about you!"

I didn't understand what he was saying; my confused reply was, "But that *is* me."

To clarify his point, he told me a story. It was about another minister who had lost touch with himself and had taken a six-month leave of absence from his congregational duties. He had decided he must "put God on the shelf"—God was no longer real to him. The Bible had become a bore. But beyond that he did not know who he was. And he knew he must find himself.

He decided that the only place to begin this quest was to start doing the things he wanted to do, not the whole world of things he had been required to do to fulfill his role of minister. But when he tried to think of what his real desires were, he could think of nothing. In his slavery to a role, he had lost the ability to savor life.

The minister without an identity drifted to men he had known only as "their minister." He went to the coffee shop where some congregated each morning before going to work. He listened to how they really thought, free of the pieties they assumed for his sake when he was a "professional preacher." He was invited to go fishing, and try his hand at pool. None of these things told him who he was, but they did let him mingle with warm, unpretentious men. He wanted that—no sham. And that is where his self-discovery began. He determined to be real, human, vulnerable, without sham, and to accept wherever that brought him. Into that new emotional climate came a fresh, deep experience of God—but not of a demanding deity he once thought God to be. He found God to be the uncoercive Spirit who lets a man just be—and in that being lies the heart of self-discovery.

I left the pastor's study still unsettled, unsure of what he was trying to tell me. But I did have the feeling that whatever it was, it had the ring of truth about it. In other words, I knew something; my heart was sure of something my mind could not yet embrace. I would just have to let whatever was trying to surface keep pecking at the shell of my old mind-set until it could hatch. That hatching process took a brief but painfully long seven months.

STOP TRYING

One Sunday I was with my family at our little cabin on a lake. I decided to take a walk alone out into the woods. As the natural beauty of this southern pine forest caressed my mind, I began to reexamine my life. What I saw was discouraging. My schedule was drudgery, my duties as a mother were confusing and dissatisfying, and worst of all, I was exhausted from the constant tyranny of being a "submissive wife." I knew the New Testament command to do just that: "Wives, submit to your husbands."[1] But I did not feel submissive, I felt coerced and taken for granted. The holy bond of matrimony felt like the bondage of servitude. I felt such a failure, so guilty and unfit to be a Christian. I wanted to scream, "Please, I can't stand being so good any more. I don't want to be religious, or a good wife, or a mother another day!"

I knelt down on the pine needles and said, "Dear heavenly Father, hear this desire of my heart. Stop this world and let me off!"

Then it was as if he asked me, "Ruth, what is your problem?"

"Lord, I am so sick and tired of trying to be a good wife—submitting and trying; I feel so trapped. I just can't go on."

"Ruth," he seemed to say, "you don't ever have to try to be a good wife again."

I didn't know what God was doing telling me a thing like that. But I felt a tremendous burden being lifted from me.

But my lament was not over. "Lord," I continued, "I am just as sick and tired of trying to be a good mother. I try so hard to serve you and then I have to try so hard to make up to my family for the days I have been away speaking about you. Then I try to overcompensate when I'm home with my children. I've got to make up for all the days it rained and I wasn't at school to pick them up."

Again, through my mind I heard him say, "Ruth, you don't ever have to try to be a good mother again."

It sounded so much as though God was indulging in heresy, but I knew it was he speaking. I felt a hundred pounds lift off my chest.

Did I dare to go on? The deep frustration I felt urged me on. "God, I'm really going to upset you this time. I'm even sicker of being a so-called 'spiritual leader' than both of those other roles put together. I have to go to meetings where everyone expects me to be 'spiritual,' to have answers, to talk right, to dress right, and to make everyone happy. I can't handle it any more!"

I heard the same gentle answer, "Ruth, you never have to try to be spiritual again." It was a strange sounding revelation. But I believed it. I rose from my knees and walked out of the woods a free woman.

For the first time I knew why Jesus said, "If the Son makes you free you will be free indeed."[2]

Reflecting on the experience, I am convinced God answered my first prayer. He let me die. I died to an old mentality which could not give expression to the real Ruth. St. Paul said what I was feeling when he wrote, "Do not be conformed to this world [with its conformist mentality] but be transformed by the renewal of your mind."[3] My mind was being renewed and I was starting to be transformed.

ACTING OUT OF THE TRUE SELF

My renewed mentality did not remove me from service to my family or to God. It let me seek out and find who I am. That was impossible as long as I was bound to the tyranny of what other people expected me to be, or even what I expected myself to be for inappropriate reasons.

What I began to see was that there were many Ruths, as there are many selves in all of us. There is the child Ruth who expects the world to satisfy her. If my inner child serves another, it is with the expectation that I should get something for my trouble. And when that something—affection, recognition, pleasure—is not forthcoming, I feel cheated or punished. My parent self can do the same thing in order to hold a position of control or power, and if that queen-of-the-mountain position is challenged or frustrated, my reaction may be anger or bitterness. The adult in me can seek a more mature relationship. But even that part of me is not the self I seek. When Simon Peter expressed concern that Jesus should not risk his life by going to Jerusalem to be murdered, he was "adult" enough. It is generally advisable to discourage deliberate, premeditated death. But Jesus faulted him because he was not responding from that higher self which understands and responds to the wisdom of the Spirit.

What frequently is lacking in humanistic psychology is this understanding. We can become "well adjusted" and simply be unconsciously resigned to lives of "quiet desperation" or noisy acceptability. We can "get along" and miss the whole point of living. Few of Jesus' contemporaries would have labeled him "well adjusted." He was disturbingly out of harmony with the people of his society. But he was not rebelling. He was not reacting to pain or responding to pleasure. Rather, he was motivated by a deep interior recognition of his relationship to the Holy Spirit and of who he really was.

No incident in his life expresses this more clearly than his washing the disciples' feet.[4] The story is introduced with these words: "Jesus, knowing that the Father had given all things into his hands, and that he had come from God and was going to God, . . . girded himself with a towel. Then he poured water into a basin, and began to wash the disciples' feet." In short that is saying, "Because Jesus knew who he was, he did what needed to be done." If he had been trying to prove that he was spiritual, he might have prayed. If he had been a status seeker, he would have tried to impress his followers. Or if he was afraid of what others might think, he would have kept track of what they most liked him to do and done that. But he had no such needs or anxieties. That freed him to follow the spiritual guidance which emanates from the true self or the soul. It allowed him to be infinitely creative and, as this story illustrates, infinitely practical.

A "Liberated" Wife

I did not know this as I walked out of the woods into a new life. I only knew that the unbearable pressure of trying to live up to what others wanted me to be, or I felt I ought to be, was taken from me.

It was like trying to walk for the first time—liberating but strange. I was out of the playpen confinement. But I was awkward and clumsy in my new walk.

As I walked back to the cabin, I heard my husband call me from the edge of the pond: "Ruth, come on down. I've caught my third fish." The family tradition was to wait until he caught three fish—which meant they were biting good—and then for him to call me to join him and "enjoy myself." Calmly, resolutely, I walked to the pier. He had always thought I liked fishing and I had been the submissive wife and had never complained. Now I heard myself saying, "I don't want to go fishing. I don't like to fish! And while I'm at it, I want you to know I can't stand playing eighteen holes of golf with you every Wednesday of my life—just because it's your day off."

He seemed a bit stunned for a moment. Then it was my turn to be surprised. He said, "This is the happiest day of my life. I thank God for this day!" Then he explained that while driving home from work at night he would think of me being home alone all day—not seeing anyone, having nothing to do. His conclusion was: women like to go to the shopping centers! "Worse than that," he went on, "has it ever dawned on you that when you're in town, for two years I haven't been able to play with my regular golf foursome on Wednesdays?"

"If the Son makes you free, you will be free indeed."[5] As I had made this first step toward my identity, Christ had prepared the path by moving my husband toward his true self. Now we agreed that when there were things he wanted to do and I did not, if after we had discussed them he still wanted to do them, I could yield to his request, but out of love rather than unwilling, but determined duty.

When the Spirit said to me in my experience in the woods, "You don't have to be a good wife," I didn't understand. It seemed so libertine, so devoid of Christian character. But what I grew to understand is that there is a diminishing return to trying to be a good wife because "I ought to." Subtle and not-so-subtle resentments begin to form. I begin to be taken for granted because I don't really bring much to a fishing trip or a round of golf if I am going out of duty. It is not the husband's fault if he is not very excited about having his wife tag along with all the enthusiasm she would feel about scrubbing woodwork. I realized that the husband is as liberated as the wife when she feels free to say no to him. If there is any communication at all, it makes her yeses much more satisfying to both parties; and the nos can allow her to be herself and allow him to relate to a wife rather than an echo.

LOVING GOD AND DOING WHAT WE WANT

This attitude can degenerate into selfishness (*I want to do what I want to do*) unless one's primary desire is to do God's will. If our goal is to do the will of God, our objective cannot be to get our own way. We are free to say no, but not if we sense it is the Spirit's purpose that we comply with our husband's wishes. When Christ is consulted in prayer and allowed to be Counselor in each decision, we will grow sensitive to the divine motivation which causes us to want to do the right thing. But approaching our relationships from this motivation brings no sense of bondage to another person. For God we can submit, even to the unpleasant task, with joy.

I find that it is my "oughts" that bring resentment and hostility. Everything that we do because we ought to causes hostility. And if we insist on being "nice," all the anger is going to come out in complaining, backbiting, or playing the moody underdog. These emotions are a monkey wrench in any marital gears.

I needed confirmation that I was not ignoring God in my flight from a domestic Egypt to the promised land of integrity in love. I found that support in the Scripture, "Delight yourself in the Lord; and He will give you the desires of your heart."[6] I saw in this promise, not that God will give me everything I want but that he will place the desires in my heart which conform to his will. Sometimes if there is something I don't want to do but feel I should, I pray, "Lord, I don't want to do this. Now Lord, if it is in your will that I do it, change my heart, change my desire." Frequently, I have the desires of my heart changed, sometimes in an instant. I consider it a wonderful, home-made miracle when the thing I most detested doing I find myself wanting to do. That is Christ changing my vinegar into honey.

At other times I have wanted to do something, such as go to an art show because I love art, but I haven't, because my past conditioning had made me believe that "if it's of the Lord, it has to hurt, and it has to be a sacrifice." But now I pray, "Lord, I want to go to this place. If it's not your will, diminish my desire. But, Lord, if it is your will, increase my desire to go."

Often there has been that increase in desire to do that fun thing and I do it. But if the desire fades, I cancel my plans. I have learned that God wants me to be happy. My happiness is in seeking first the kingdom of God, not submissive wifery. When I seek that authentic identity which the kingdom of God creates, submission to God without slavery is the natural product.

LIBERATED MOTHERHOOD

Erma Bombeck divides suburban mothers into two categories: the Super Moms and the Interim Moms. Super Moms, as she describes them, keep their homes looking like something out of *House Beautiful* while they are remodeling. They keep their kids and their floors spotless, belong to all the right clubs, are civic minded, and can be at three appointments in an hour with not a hair out of place.

Interim Moms just hang on until their kids grow up.

I was a Semi-Super Mom. As my work expanded and I was invited to other cities, in my absence my children were left in the care of our housekeeper. Whenever I returned, I tried to make up for those days away. I began to overcompensate. For instance if I had an appointment with the dentist and my daughter had an art lesson, the moment she asked me to take her I would forget the personal appointment and chauffeur her to and from her destination. This was not being selfless. At that point I was not denying myself, I was trying to reestablish the esteem of my children. So, in a sense, although my actions were sacrificial, they were self-serving. I wanted to be a Super Mom to my children.

However, in the whirl of service to my children I was denying them the right to have a real mother, and I was denying me the right to be me. And at last the puzzling words spoken to my heart by God made sense. "You don't ever have to be a good mother again." He was not saying I had the right to neglect my children or abuse them. He was saying, "Relax. There is so much I can do for your children through you, if you will stop trying so hard. One minute of my Spirit touching your sons and daughters through you is worth more than days of being a busy, slavish Super Mom."

This insight began to change my approach to my children. I said to them, "All right, if you want me to do something for you that will require a lot of time, I want to know twenty-four hours in advance. And no more last-minute buying sprees. From now on we'll shop one day out of every month and from a planned shopping list." I discovered I had bought socks and underwear and too many dresses to pay for my time away from them. To them this part of the revolution in me was revolting.

Shortly after my announcement, I was out in the back yard relaxing when my daughter came running out. "Mother, Mother. Come on! We have to go down to the Motor Vehicle Department and get my driver's license!"

With my heart going ninety miles an hour and my voice idling, I said, "Well, Honey, you didn't put it on the schedule, and I have it on my schedule to take this time out for a sunbath."

"But Mother, I've been waiting sixteen years!"

That hurt. But I persevered, "Well," I said, "you're

going to wait sixteen years and one day, or, you're going to get somebody else to take you. I'm taking a sunbath."

That was the least enjoyable sunbath of my whole life. But, just perhaps, it was the most rewarding.

My children and I are still in the process of reconstructing our relationships. There have been mutual misunderstandings, but these were beneficial and rewarding because they required that we talk things through. This has moved us closer together without the need to intrude on each other's legitimate independence. The time wasted indulging our children has given way to a more creative give and take.

Gradually out of a maze of negative emotions—duty, guilt, fear—I moved into the positive privilege of motherhood. Now the emotion I had known faintly all along, namely service out of caring, became the dominant emotion in my relationship with my children.

Mutual respect was a hard lesson for the children to learn. And many times I felt selfish because I would not drop what I was doing to attend to them. But this guilt feeling faded as I saw how my release stimulated their sense of responsibility. Scheduling forced them to consider others when making their plans.

My old Super Mom complex would surface on occasion. I would try to be everywhere at once, leaping over tall demands with a single bound for my children. But usually I would correct my compulsion to be their slave before they could get very far into any new bad habits of parent abuse.

FROM PEDESTAL TO PERSON

The most difficult area of my life to express the freedom the Spirit had given me was the religious. I was the teacher of a Bible class and had worked hard at being "the spiritual leader." That demanded, I felt, that I be an inexhaustible source of insights and inspiration. And if I didn't have any insights, I would stay up half the night before our next meeting looking for some. When I entered the room, everyone would gather around and wait for me to perform. And I would perform.

They expected me to feed them and I did. I performed because I wanted to stay on the pedestal on which they had placed me. My pedestal-posing was not conscious. As with every sincere Christian, I consciously wanted to be humble. But unconsciously I needed the glory, the pat on the back, the assurance from them that they could not get along without me. My role was that of a performing caged lion. When they said "Jump on the pedestal," I jumped. I wanted them to think of me as Saint Ruth. Unfortunately, my halo was too small and my head too big. And consequently the religious role became an unbearable headache.

As I saw how precarious and painful it was to be on a pedestal, I willed to come down and be a person. I told my Bible class that they no longer had a teacher and a leader. We were all equal members of the body of Christ; all should be ready to contribute their insight and experience to the class. The women sat in silence for five minutes staring at me. I desperately wanted to fill the painful quiet with my words but I knew I must not.

A little voice from way back in the room said, "You know, Ruth, I feel that the Lord wants me to pray for you. But who am I to pray for you?"

"Peggy," I replied, "you are just as worthy as any to pray, and I'll tell you why the Lord wants you to pray for me. I've been suffering, on and off, for two months with terrible sinus pain, and I've been too proud to let you, or anyone, know. I was afraid you might think less of me, as though my sinus condition was caused by sin in my life."

"But Ruth," she said, "I don't know how to pray."

I walked over, knelt down in front of her, and said, "Honey, put your hand right there where it hurts." I placed her hand across my right cheek. "Jesus," she stammered, "heal Ruth." The moment she uttered those words, my pain was gone completely!

Since that experience I have wondered how many Christians are kept in a spiritual crib because sincere religious leaders are bound to the role of a guru. What the people need is a vulnerable equal who needs them as much as and sometimes more than they need him or her.

In each of my roles as wife, mother, and religious leader I became aware of things in my past which instigated the unhealthy role-playing that obscured my real identity. I saw how childhood rejection subtly and subconsciously forced me into an inordinate quest for acceptance, a need to protect myself from further rejection. Most frequently this pattern manifested itself in a need to be accepted by my husband, my children, and my social and spiritual group. I suffered from a common human malady: fear that I would not be loved if people really knew me as I was. When I dropped my masks, I was amazed to find that most people accepted the vulnerable, self-confessed imperfect me more than the unreal St. Ruth. They could communicate with a blemished but real person.

It is wonderful to discover that we don't have to pretend that we are paragons of virtue. It is more wonderful to let this knowledge release us from the pressures of pretense. There is gratifying freedom in breaking out of the molds that we have allowed our environments to put us in. We have to dare to be ourselves. We have to do things that are the expression of what God created us to be rather than what fear and selfishness compel us to do.

FREE TO BE HAPPY

Some might think that if we break out of the mold and are released from pressures that we will become terribly self-indulgent. This will not happen if our primary desire is to do the will of God, because the Spirit will not let us enjoy selfishness. Even though we have the freedom to do something selfish, Jesus keeps us in touch with our true self and reveals an area of weakness that we can release to him for healing. "Whoever has the will to do the will of God shall know."[7] A self-indulgent person, by definition, does not seek the will of God.

Our puritanical roots make it difficult for us to believe that God is a God of fun. So, we have to trust the Spirit to teach us how to have fun, how to take relaxed, nonbusiness time for ourselves. As we keep open, the inner guidance will tell us the things which we should, or should not, be doing. We are physically and emotionally constructed to enjoy the spiritually creative. Dr. E. Stanley Jones observed that everyone has a Christian body: by this he meant that all bodies thrive on the emotions which emerge from the loving heart of God, such as love and joy. Stomach ulcers are the product of too much pressure, usually caused by the demand to achieve more than we feel capable of achieving. The body is saying that it needs the peace and unconditional approval of God; it needs more relaxation.

If we would listen to what our bodies are saying with the inner hearing made sensitive by the Spirit we would be shown the kind of correction and changes of pace we need. And all of life would become so much more fun. Some people do need to have their self-indulgence curbed. But at this point in my experience, I needed to be set free to enjoy neglected needs and desires of my heart. There are many Christians who are in this same condition: they need to be unshackled.

I remember sitting on a plane, returning home from one more series of meetings and people, people, people. I put my tired head back and thought about how much I would enjoy the total indulgence of doing nothing. I had the overwhelming desire to collapse into a tub of warm water and then slip into my worn-out, comfortable robe. Then in this fantasy induced by fatigue, I saw my feet propped up, while I dozed off intermittently in front of the TV.

As I walked into the house, the phone was ringing. It was a friend of mine, the pastor of a local church. He had arranged a convocation of four churches for that evening and had been anxiously awaiting my arrival home to inform me that at last I would be able to meet with these leaders and give instruction as to how small groups could be formed. This was for him a dream of ten years come true.

But I had a conflicting dream. I felt the God who made my body wanted me to be done with ministering for a short while. So I said firmly, "It's impossible for me tonight. I've already made plans. I will do it any other night. I wish you had let me know . . ."

"But, there's no way we can change to another night. It's all planned. We postponed it once awaiting your return."

I told him I would see what I could do.

As I hung up the phone, twenty years of conditioning—always serve others first, be self-sacrificing, be unselfish, recognize that church work must come before pleasure always, other's needs are always more important than mine—almost demoralized me.

As I reached for the phone again to accept the pastor's invitation, I was arrested by the question, "Am I being true to the freedom Christ has just given me?" I knew I had to pray. With all my heart I prayed, "God, if I am to go, give me at least some little desire to minister tonight." Then I sat back, quietly monitoring my feelings. The desire for that warm bath and that pleasurable but seemingly useless night of TV intensified. I waited. I really had expected God to give me the grace to go. Eventually, I realized that I was not to go. God wanted the temple of his Spirit, my body, to be prepared for future service. And that required complete rest that night!

When I called the pastor to inform him that it was impossible to change my plans, he asked me if I could suggest a stand-in. Immediately, four ladies from my Bible class came to mind, and I gave their names and phone numbers to him.

Within an hour each of the four called to tell me, nervously, what time they would pick me up. Their disappointment and disapproval exceeded the pastor's when I told them I could not and would not be going.

"But, Ruth, we can't do this without you," said one, expressing the fear of all.

I was feeling as much a traitor to them as they

were feeling abandoned. But in my heart I knew, somehow, I was being obedient to the Spirit.

My night of relaxation was only interrupted once. The door bell rang just before midnight. I roused myself from bed and found my four "stand-ins" at the door, their faces all aglow.

"He did it, Ruth—Christ did it!" one of them exclaimed.

They shared with me the joy and exhilaration of seeing how God could use even them. They had prayed for the sick. Others had committed their lives to the service of Christ. One old man had tearfully, joyously accepted Christ into his heart for the first time.

Each woman had spoken publicly for the first time. Each had supported the other when one was leading. When the convocation had split into four groups, each had been appointed as leader of a group. Alone they experienced the same sense of divine support and guidance. This was the beginning of a new productive ministry for each one.

Now wasn't that amazing! I wanted to rest, God wanted me to rest, and he took care of everything. It was as if God had said to me, "Ruth, trust me. When you do, your fun and relaxation are as important to me as your more serious service."

As long as we seek first God's kingdom and act within his love, he will provide the necessary balance between easy living and hard labor.

DON'T LET THE WORLD SMOTHER YOUR UNIQUENESS

As no two flowers or snowflakes are the same, so no two people have been created alike. Therefore we should not expect others to express themselves in the same way. God has so many beautiful things to say that it requires the existence of every person in the world to begin to express the infinite variety of his nature. To imitate another or to slavishly obey another's direction can distort our basic nature. And that really distorts the image of God. The truest expression of ourselves is not governed by morality. It is realized by allowing a truer revelation of God in us.

If we follow Paul's instruction and do not let the world squeeze us into its mold, but let God remold our minds from within,[8] we cannot look to other people for guidelines. We must look within. That is where the blueprint of our life is to be found. The making of the new heart and the right spirit within us is the work of God.[9] It is a work that must come from within through healing love which allows a clearer, truer self-image to form. We have been so conditioned to take advice—all too readily offered—from society and significant friends. The advice may be wise and benevolently given. But it is not necessarily God's guidance for *us*. So, all advice must be taken with a grain of faith—faith in God's guidance rather than man's.

It is natural to want to be a good mate, a good parent, to be professionally successful and an upstanding citizen. However, the harder we work at this with our eyes on a human rather than a divine standard, the more intense our feelings of failure or frustration will become.

Not only will we have to live with the feelings of failure generated by standards which don't fit our blueprint, we will also have to deal with growing resentment over the pressure of what we feel others are requiring us to do. These resentments usually begin as boredom or hatred for one's livelihood and social activities. Ultimately they are shifted to the people who have influenced us to do the distasteful things. Unfortunately, these people are usually close family members, or church and business associates. Once the pressure of resentments gets heavy, creative relationships are impossible. A vicious circle begins. Resentment depletes the ability to love, declining love destroys relationships, broken relationships create guilt. The guilt unrelieved causes one to resent others in an effort to be free of the pain of the guilt.

We cannot escape this cycle as long as we allow the world, even our Christian friends, to squeeze us into a role we were not meant to play. In letting go and being ourselves, we begin a new joy in the Christian life. We begin to be free and happy.

Being Open to Change

It is a delightful revelation to see how God changes the desires of our heart when our will is to do his will.

One week in the midst of a very busy schedule I had set aside Saturday and Sunday to be with my family. My husband and my two teenage children had equally busy schedules. We decided to get away together to Myrtle Beach. But when I phoned for reservations I was told that because it was Mother's Day and there was an annual statewide hospital convention, every available room had been reserved months in advance. Several other calls confirmed what the first reservation clerk had said. Just when it seemed that our family getaway was to be scrubbed, I made one last call with a dial and a prayer. When I gave my name, the stranger on the other end said,

"Are you the same Ruth Stapleton scheduled to speak at the retreat in a few weeks? I got a brochure on it just today."

When I said that I was, she responded, "Oh, I'm so glad. These weekends are so wild; we really need praying people down here. If you'll just come, I'll find places for your family, even if it's on my kitchen floor."

We arrived to find ourselves accommodated in royal style: an ocean front apartment with veranda overlooking a swimming pool and patio. I was so grateful to God for taking care of us in such a beautiful way. All I had to do for two days was to lie on the beach, relax in surf or pool, and bask in the love of my family.

Shortly after our arrival I went to the office to introduce myself and express my gratitude to the woman who had arranged for this blissful weekend. She was doubly happy to see me because she had great news to share: all of her praying Christian friends had been invited to her house at eight o'clock that Saturday night to meet me, to share, and to minister to each other!

"But, this is impossible," I said. "I've already made other plans. I wish I had known . . . If you'd only let me know . . ."

"Do you mean to tell me that I've got to call everybody and cancel this meeting?" was her response.

"It's impossible for me to go. I've made a commitment to my family."

This commitment, made in the car on the way to Myrtle Beach, was to see a motion picture and go to dinner at our favorite Myrtle Beach restaurant. I didn't tell her the nature of my commitment. But I so wanted to be with my family.

When she saw that I was determined, she was disappointed and even a little angry. I felt compelled to say, "Obviously this is a matter which requires prayer. Don't cancel the meeting for at least an hour."

My husband freed me by saying, "This is your vacation; you do whatever you want."

I changed into my bathing suit and went to the beach still very committed to spending this weekend with my family.

Though I felt the conflict of my obligation to serve and the social obligation of returning a favor to my benefactress, I was confident that my decision would not be changed. Muttering inwardly, "Lord, not my will but thy will," I relaxed in the sun. Then strange thoughts intruded. I had never thought about the Christians at Myrtle Beach. Who were they? What were they like? Did they need any help I could render? Had they ever heard of inner healing or the baptism of the Holy Spirit? Suddenly, I had to know the answers firsthand. I jumped to my feet and hurried toward the office, hoping that I wasn't too late to catch her before she canceled the meeting.

I wasn't. To her delight and mine we made arrangements to get to the meeting.

As I walked away from the office, I was overwhelmed with the realization that the desire of my heart had been changed; there was no demand, just desire, God-inspired desire.

When I went into the motel room to discuss the change in plans, my thirteen-year-old son, Michael, was talking to his father, asking permission to go with a new friend to eat a TV dinner at their apartment and watch television instead of going with the family to a movie and dinner.

Returning to the beach, I was hardly surprised

when Patti, my sixteen-year-old, said, "Now Mother, don't you get upset by what I'm going to say. Wait till I finish before you give me your answer. There's this boy . . . he's so darling. And I know you don't know him, he's a stranger. But he asked me for a date tonight to go swimming and for dinner, and I'd really like to go. You know, I'd really rather do this than anything in the world."

I smiled internally at God's humor in handling my children in this way, while I granted her permission to go out.

All oughts had been eliminated. I was doing what I wanted to do.

My desires had been changed. The meeting that night lasted from eight until well past midnight. And the experience was the highlight of my weekend.

A safe guideline for freedom without license is that if God does not change our desires and if it does not contradict scripture, or the divine definition of love found in Jesus Christ, then we are free to do as we desire. This freedom to be oneself demands a will absolutely committed to doing the will of God. But this, after all, is our highest obligation and our greatest privilege.

NOTES

Introduction
1. Luke 4:18, Amplified.
2. Matt. 15:18.
3. Rom. 8:18–22, NEB.

Chapter 1: *The Healing Power of Love*
1. Luke 23:33–34.
2. Exod. 20:5.
3. Rom. 12:2, KJV.
4. Matt. 12:20.
5. John 8:12.
6. 2 Pet. 3:8, KJV.
7. Isa. 65:24.
8. John 8:58.
9. The term most commonly used is *unconscious,* but I prefer to use the term *subconscious.*
10. Matt. 12:34–35, JB.
11. Luke 1:44.
12. Ps. 139.
13. 1 John 4:8.
14. 1 Cor. 13:7.
15. 1 Cor. 14:1.

The Experience of Inner Healing

Chapter 2: *The Healing Power of Faith*
1. Matt. 13:58.
2. Mark 4:28.
3. Rom. 10:17, NAS.
4. John 14:13; 15:7; 16:24.
5. Phil. 3:10.
6. "He [God] has forgiven you all your sins: Christ has utterly wiped out the damning evidence of broken laws and commandments which always hung over our heads. . . . And then, having drawn the sting of all the powers ranged against us, he exposed them, shattered, empty and defeated, in his final glorious triumphant act!" (Col. 2:13–15, Phillips.)
7. Heb. 12:1–2.

Chapter 3: *The Healing Power of Surrender*
1. Deut. 33:27, KJV & RSV.
2. Luke 5:31–32.
3. Mark 12:37.
4. John 8:32.
5. John 14:9.
6. Luke 7:36–50.
7. Matt. 6:19–20.
8. Eph. 5:18.
9. Napoleon Hill, *Think and Grow Rich* (New York: Hawthorn, 1966).
10. John 7:37.

Chapter 4: *The Healing Power of Forgiveness*
1. John 13:27.
2. Matt. 6:11.
3. John 16:13.
4. Matt. 18:22.
5. Pss. 135:13–16; 23:1.
6. Isa. 55.

Chapter 5: *The Healing Power of Confession*
1. Luke 18:9–14.
2. See Matt. 9:11–13; John 9:39–41.
3. John 20:22–23.
4. Luke 5:19–25.
5. James 5:16.
6. 1 John 1:9.
7. 1 John 4:18.
8. Job 3:25, KJV.
9. Rom. 3:23, KJV.

Notes

Chapter 6: *The Healing Power of Self-Acceptance*
1. Heb. 12:2.
2. John 21:15–17.
3. 2 Cor. 5:21.
4. John 21:15–19. In the Greek two different words for love are used.
5. Jer. 32:26.

Chapter 7: *The Healing Power of Release*
1. Deut. 33:27.
2. 2 Chron. 20:17.
3. Matt. 5:6.

Chapter 8: *The Healing Power of Purpose*
1. Matt. 10:38.
2. Ps. 32:8.
3. Matt. 6:33; John 15:12; Luke 10:27.
4. Rom. 5:5.
5. Faith is "the evidence of things not seen" according to Heb. 11:1, KJV.
6. 1 Cor. 2:8.
7. Phil. 4:6; 1 Thess. 5:18, NAS.
8. Rom. 8:37.
9. Ps. 139.
10. Gal. 5:22-23.

Chapter 9: *The Healing Power of Serving*
1. See John 10:10.
2. See Luke 22:34, 32. LB.
3. See Isa. 6:8.
4. Matt. 18:19, NIV.
5. Matt. 5:28–33.
6. 1 Cor. 12.
7. Luke 17:33, NEB.
8. Matt. 13:3–9.
9. Phil. 2:9–10.
10. Matt. 20:28.

Chapter 10: *The Healing Power of Listening*
1. Mark 8:18; Jer. 5:21; Ezek. 12:2; Matt. 13:14–15; Isa. 6:9–10; Pss. 115:4–8; 135:15–18.
2. John 20:22. It is noteworthy that both in Hebrew and Greek the words for *inspiration* and *breath* are identical: *pneuma* in Greek and *nephesh* in Hebrew.
3. Ps. 91:1, KJV.

4. Matt. 6:25–33.
5. Gal. 6:7.
6. Phil. 4:8.
7. 2 Cor. 10:5, Phillips.

Chapter 11: *The Healing Power of Adversity*
1. Matt. 5:3.
2. Acts 17:28.
3. Deut. 33:27.
4. Matt. 7:6.

Chapter 12: *The Healing Power of Authentic Self-Identity*
1. Eph. 5:22.
2. John 8:36.
3. Rom. 12:2.
4. John 13:3–5.
5. John 8:36.
6. Ps. 37:11, NAS.
7. John 7:17, NEB.
8. Rom. 12:2, Phillips.
9. Ps. 51:10.

ABOUT THE AUTHOR

RUTH STAPLETON has been in constant demand as a speaker on inner healing and has fulfilled an extensive number of speaking engagements in the United States. She holds an M.A.T. degree from the University of North Carolina and currently serves as president of Behold, Inc., a nondenominational healing corporation. In addition she has conducted healing and teaching missions in England, Canada, Australia and New Zealand, Israel, Portugal, Japan and other Far Eastern countries. Mrs. Stapleton and her husband, Robert, make their home in Fayetteville, North Carolina. They have four children.

INSPIRATIONAL FAVORITES

EUGENIA PRICE

St. Simon's Trilogy

☐	10495	Beloved Invader	$1.75
☐	11189	New Moon Rising	$1.75
☐	12717	Lighthouse	$1.95
		and	
☐	6485	Don Juan McQueen	$1.75
☐	8878	Woman To Woman	$1.50

HAL LINDSEY

☐	11545	The Liberation of Planet Earth	$1.95
☐	11132	Satan Is Alive And Well On Planet Earth	$1.95
☐	11259	The Terminal Generation	$1.95
☐	10382	There's A New World Coming	$1.95

Buy them at your local bookstore or use this handy coupon for ordering:

Heartwarming Books
of
Faith and Inspiration

☐	11710	**THE GOSPEL ACCORDING TO PEANUTS** Robert L. Short	$1.50
☐	2576	**HOW CAN I FIND YOU, GOD?** Marjorie Holmes	$1.75
☐	10947	**THE FINDING OF JASPER HOLT** Grace Livingston Hill	$1.50
☐	10176	**THE BIBLE AS HISTORY** Werner Keller	$2.50
☐	12218	**THE GREATEST MIRACLE IN THE WORLD** Og Mandino	$1.95
☐	2866	**THE WOMAN AT THE WELL** Dale Evans Rogers	$1.50
☐	12009	**THE GREATEST SALESMAN IN THE WORLD** Og Mandino	$1.95
☐	12330	**I'VE GOT TO TALK TO SOMEBODY, GOD** Marjorie Holmes	$1.95
☐	10291	**THE GIFT OF INNER HEALING** Ruth Carter Stapleton	$1.75
☐	12444	**BORN AGAIN** Charles Colson	$2.50
☐	11012	**FASCINATING WOMANHOOD** Helen Andelin	$1.95
☐	12066	**TWO FROM GALILEE** Marjorie Holmes	$1.95
☐	12717	**LIGHTHOUSE** Eugenia Price	$1.95
☐	12835	**NEW MOON RISING** Eugenia Price	$1.95
☐	11291	**THE LATE GREAT PLANET EARTH** Hal Lindsey	$1.95
☐	11140	**REFLECTIONS ON LIFE AFTER LIFE** Dr. Raymond Moody	$1.95

Buy them at your local bookstore or use this handy coupon for ordering:

Bantam Books, Inc., Dept. HF, 414 East Golf Road, Des Plaines, Ill. 60016

Please send me the books I have checked above. I am enclosing $_____
(please add 7¢ to cover postage and handling). Send check or money order
—no cash or C.O.D.'s please.

Mr/Mrs/Miss _____

Address _____

City _____ State/Zip _____

HF—1/79

Please allow four weeks for delivery. This offer expires 7/79.

RELAX!
SIT DOWN
and Catch Up On Your Reading!

☐	11877	**HOLOCAUST** by Gerald Green	$2.25
☐	12836	**THE CHANCELLOR MANUSCRIPT**	$2.75
		by Robert Ludlum	
☐	10077	**TRINITY** by Leon Uris	$2.75
☐	2300	**THE MONEYCHANGERS** by Arthur Hailey	$1.95
☐	12550	**THE MEDITERRANEAN CAPER**	$2.25
		by Clive Cussler	
☐	11469	**AN EXCHANGE OF EAGLES** by Owen Sela	$2.25
☐	2600	**RAGTIME** by E. L. Doctorow	$2.25
☐	11428	**FAIRYTALES** by Cynthia Freeman	$2.25
☐	11966	**THE ODESSA FILE** by Frederick Forsyth	$2.25
☐	11557	**BLOOD RED ROSES** by Elizabeth B. Coker	$2.25
☐	11708	**JAWS 2** by Hank Searls	$2.25
☐	12490	**TINKER, TAILOR, SOLDIER, SPY**	$2.50
		by John Le Carre	
☐	11929	**THE DOGS OF WAR** by Frederick Forsyth	$2.25
☐	10526	**INDIA ALLEN** by Elizabeth B. Coker	$1.95
☐	12489	**THE HARRAD EXPERIMENT**	$2.25
		by Robert Rimmer	
☐	11767	**IMPERIAL 109** by Richard Doyle	$2.50
☐	10500	**DOLORES** by Jacqueline Susann	$1.95
☐	11601	**THE LOVE MACHINE** by Jacqueline Susann	$2.25
☐	11886	**PROFESSOR OF DESIRE** by Philip Roth	$2.50
☐	10857	**THE DAY OF THE JACKAL**	$1.95
		by Frederick Forsyth	
☐	11952	**DRAGONARD** by Rupert Gilchrist	$1.95
☐	11331	**THE HAIGERLOCH PROJECT** by Ib Melchior	$2.25
☐	11330	**THE BEGGARS ARE COMING** by Mary Loos	$1.95

Buy them at your local bookstore or use this handy coupon for ordering: